GOD'S SENSE OF HUMOR
—WHERE?
—WHEN?
—HOW?

GOD'S SENSE
OF
HUMOR
–WHERE?
–WHEN?
–HOW?

by
The Rev. Dr. Bob Parrott

Philosophical Library
New York

Library of Congress Cataloging in Publication Data

Parrott, Bob W.
  God's sense of humor—where?—when?—how?

  1. Wit and humor—Religious aspects—Christianity.
2. Pastoral theology. I. Title.
BV4013.P37 1983   253   82-24637
ISBN 0-8022-2421-0

Copyright. 1984. by Philosophical Library. Inc.
200 West 57th Street. New York. N.Y. 10019
Manufactured in the United States of America

TO

Our daughter Deborah
whose sense of humor blesses
her father as does no other.

Contents

Preface xi

PART I: Humor in the Preacher

  A. You Need to Understand How Humor
       Works 3

  B. God Laughs at and with Us 9

  C. God Saves the Preacher Through Good
       Humor..............................11

  D. The Comic and the Good-Humored
       Preacher 21

  E. The Preacher Goes Beyond Humor
       to God 24

  F. The Ultimate Example of Humor Comes
       Through Jesus Christ 31

PART II: Humor in Devotions

  A. In Your Devotional Bible Study You Can
       See Your Own Incongruities 41

  B. The Prayer Time in Our Devotions May
       Actually Begin with an Incongruity 46

  C. The Demonic Destroyer of the Human
       Spirit is Self-Deception.................51

  D. Pray to Know the Truth of God 52

  E. Your Devotion Time Is a Time Set Aside
       for God 59

PART III: **Humor in Pastoral Care**

    A.   A Metaphysical Definition of Pastoral
          Care Is in Order 65

    B.   Incongruities Exist Within the Fabric of
          These Tragic Settings 70

    C.   Truth Therapy Is the Most Powerful
          Therapy of All 71

    D.   The Pastor Expresses Care by Being in
          the Presence of Another 85

PART IV: **Humor in the Order of Worship**

    A.   Two Terms May be Used Interchangeably—
          Liturgy and Ritual 91

    B.   A Means by Which a Congregation
          Worships God 93

    C.   Liturgies Must Be Adapted to the
          Situation 97

    D.   "When Two or More Gather In My Name,
          I Will Be There" 101

    E.   Some Parts of Liturgy Are Always Being
          Debated 107

    F.   There Is No Place for Intended Humor
          in the Order of Worship 116

PART V: **Humor in Preparing the Sermon**

    A.   Lack of Adequate Sermon Preparation
          May Cause Unintended Humor 129

    B.   Possibilities of Success—That Is the Best
          You Can Hope For 132

    C.   Some Guidelines to Keep in Mind When
          Planning the Sermon 134

    D.   Look for the Right Places in the Sermon
          to Plan for the Use of Humor 139

    E.   These Guidelines and Suggestions Can
          Help You Study Your Use of Humor 165

PART VI: **Humor in the Pulpit-Preaching Situation**

    A. The Testing Place 169
    B. Model for the Pulpit-Preaching
          Situation 171
    C. Noise Disrupts 179
    D. The Use of Humor is Risky Business 189

Postscript 195

Notes 201

PREFACE

This "how to" book is grounded in the theology/meta-physics of *Ontology of Humor*, published in 1982 by the Philosophical Library. The Use of *God's Sense of Humor* transfers the metaphysics of humor into the situation where humor is used in the preacher's witness. This book becomes for the preacher a guide in the use of humor for the total witnessing situation. The total situation in this writing includes God's sense of humor in the preacher, in his/her devotions, in pastoral care, in the order of worship, in sermon preparation, and in the pulpit-preaching situation.

Behavioral scientist Charles G. Blewitt stated in his review of *Ontology of Humor:* "Parrott's approach to his subject is non-scientific. Throughout we are offered many cogent remarks by learned theologians, but there is very little substantive scientific information about the emotional mechanics involved with humor. Here Parrott's 'Ontology' is its weakest. He sees in extremely judgmental fashion all humor as externally directed through the Creator." (*Best Sellers,* Vol. 42, Number 5, August 1982, pp. 197-8.) The reviewer offers a bit of unintended humor. He sees himself being "scientific" in his put-down of the Creator's involvement in a creation that includes humor. And he does it in an "extremely judgmental fashion"! When he penned that statement, surely a Heavenly chuckle trickled across the cosmos.

As *Ontology of Humor* acknowledges that all meaning and purpose come through Being-itself (God), so does *God's Sense of Humor*. Only the heart of faith can comprehend its meaning. It is a strange and wonderful mystery that the heart of faith can traffic in the reasoning of the world (humanism/behavioral science), but the world cannot fathom the thoughts that issue from faith.

While this book is dedicated to our daughter Deborah, it is written to the honor and glory of God. Essentially, it is His book. Only with Him does it make sense for the writer and the reader.

My gratitude goes to those whose incongruities found their way into the book through illustrations of humor (situations that might cause embarrassment have been altered to protect the privacy of persons). Throughout my ministry I have kept negatively oriented letters. I prefer letters of affirmation and thank God for them! However, these negative comments have a way of keeping me better balanced in my thinking about myself. My gratitude goes to Joe Johnson, who encouraged me to write the book, and who expressed confidence in my ability to teach preachers how to utilize humor in their preaching; to George Hunter III, who exposed me to communications insights that influenced greatly Parts V and VI of the book; to my secretary, Ms. Eloise Wilson, who typed and retyped the book, and in the process edited it; to my wife, who contributed by listening, commenting, editing, and sometimes taking dictation as I drove down the highway or flew our plane across the sky; to our daughter Deborah, who also edited the book; and to the Cosmic Ironist, Being-itself, who sifted these thoughts through my mind, and gave the insights that made the book possible. The mistakes belong to me. The Truths belong to Him, including the Truth that reveals my mistakes!

Acknowledgments

The author wishes to gratefully acknowledge permission to quote from the following sources:

Comic Laughter, by Marie Collins Swakey (New Haven: Yale University Press, 1961).

The Enjoyment of Laughter, by Max Eastman (New York: Simon & Schuster, 1936).

The Humorous Mr. Lincoln, by Keith W. Jennison (New York: Bonanza Books, 1965).

Payday Everyday, by Robert G. Lee (Nashville: Broadman Press, 1947), p. 106, 107.

Preacher, You're the Best Pasture We've Ever Had, by Joe Johnson (Nashville: Broadman Press, 1972), pp. 9, 14, 23, 25, 26, 29.

Preaching the Good News, by George E. Sweazey (Englewood Cliffs, N.J.: Prentice-Hall, Inc., 1976).

GOD'S SENSE OF HUMOR
—WHERE?
—WHEN?
—HOW?

PART I

HUMOR IN
THE PREACHER

HUMOR IN
THE PREACHER

A. Before you can know how humor works in the preach-er, *you need to understand how humor works* in anybody. Max Eastman describes finite humor this way:

> It seems to me just here that nature, in her necessity to make us happy when we play—by what interior means we can hardly guess—has triumphed over the very terms of life. For she has ordained it in the inmost structure of our minds that playful dreadfulness instead of hurting makes us laugh. Indeed it is the first sure sign of play in babies when they giggle instead of looking troubled at our gargoyle faces, and when they find amusement in our snatching away a thing they have reached out to grasp. That feeling of amusement is a new, unique one, and that giggle is a different act from the smile of grati-fication which greets a friendly look. It is an act of wel-coming a playful shock of disappointment. . . . It is an instinct. . . . and this instinct is the germ and simple rudiment of what we call the sense of humor. . . . That humorous laughter belongs among the hereditary in-stincts is indicated by the fact that it appears so early and so spontaneously. We never have to teach children

3

when to laugh; we have to teach them when not to laugh.[1]

Max Eastman shows how this finite humor comes across in two different ways:

The next time you are called upon to entertain a baby, I will tell you what to do. Laugh, and then make a perfectly terrible face. If the baby is old enough to perceive faces, and properly equipped for the calamities of the life that lies before him, he will laugh too. But if you make a perfectly terrible face all of a sudden without laughing, he is more likely to scream with fright. In order to laugh at a frightful thing he has to be in a mood of play.

If that perceptual effort is beyond him, try a practical joke. Offer him something that he wants a little and will reach out to get, and when he is about to grasp it, jerk it *smilingly away*. Again he may set up a yell of indignation, or he may emit a rollicking and extreme cackle, a kind of kicking scream, as though at the most ingenious joke ever perpetrated since Adam lost a rib.

Those are the two orthodox ways of entertaining a baby. And they correspond to two of the most famous definitions of the comic ever given. Aristotle defined the comic as "some defect or ugliness which is not painful or destructive," and added: "For example, the comic mask is ugly and distorted but does not cause pain." In other words, it is *making terrible faces playfully*.

. . . Another famous philosopher, Immanuel Kant, defined the cause of laughter as "The sudden transformation of a strained expectation into nothing"—or in other words, *as reaching after something and finding that it is not there*.[2]

4

In the first expression of humor the baby saw the incongruity between the two faces in a playful spirit. In the second expression of humor came the element of surprise. What was expected changed to something totally different. The first funny-looking incongruity (ludicrous) amused; the second rug-pulling incongruity (witty) surprised. In both cases the baby laughed in good humor.

> Practical jokes, for instance, have to start off *plausibly* and collapse *suddenly.* A ludicrous impression can be preposterous right from the start, if the comedian has your interested attention; and suddenness, although it may add a charm, is wholly unessential to it. "Neatness," so almost absolute a law for practical jokes, would be the strangulation of poetic humor. And "timing," although it has a value in all arts, is not the crucial thing in painting funny pictures that it is in making witty cracks.[2a]

We react to these two basic kinds of incongruities when Truth illumines the gap between what was and now is, between the familiar and the different experiences. When you add man's sin through his pride to these finite incongruities, the resulting incongruities (man is not who he ought to be when he acts like what he is not) create ambiguities *ad infinitum.* These sin-caused incongruities reveal the tragic dimensions of human existence.

Malcolm Muggeridge, past editor of the English humorous magazine *Punch,* spoke in our local church. He said to our congregation, "People are infinitely more humorous than anything I could think up. Following a performance of *Godspell* the Archbishop of Canterbury jumped up and said, 'Long live God!' " Muggeridge continued, "That's like saying, 'Long live Eternity!' or 'Keep it up Infinity!' " What is funnier than that? Laughter is not just a way of being amused. It is that. But it also gives tremendous illuminations of life. Muggeridge said:

> I came to this conclusion ultimately. Humor is the fantastic disparity between human aspiration and human performance. As such it is not just something that makes you laugh, but is a real comment on human life. The earliest form of humor is the joke about sex. Because if there is one activity in this life that illustrates the disparity between human aspiration and human performance, it is surely that. Sex is a joke. As a matter of fact, it is a joke that gets funnier and funnier as you get older![3]

Let us look at a few ways that humor works:
1. The closer we are to these tragic dimensions of incongruities, the more likely for tears to flow. The gap of the incongruity closes, and you grieve. *At a distance the gap opens,* and now you laugh midst your tears.

> Humor finds its basis in the incongruity of life itself, the contrast between the fretting cares and the petty sorrows of the day and the long mystery of the tomorrow. Here laughter and tears become one, and the humor becomes the contemplation and interpretation of our life.[4]

For instance, a dry alcoholic may laugh at his wet alcoholic antics—at the time he hid the bottle when he quit drinking just in case he wanted to start again! But when he hid the bottle, he was not laughing. He was too involved in the tragedy to laugh.

Victor Frankl describes his laughter through tears this way:

Humor was another of the soul's weapons in the fight for self-preservation. It is well known that humor, more than anything else in the human makeup, can afford an aloofness and an ability to rise above any situation, even if only for a few seconds. I practically trained a friend of mine who worked next to me on the building site to develop a sense of humor. I suggested to him that we would promise each other to invent at least one amusing story daily, about some incident that could happen one day after our liberation. He was a surgeon and had been an assistant on the staff of a large hospital. So I once tried to get him to smile by describing to him how he would be unable to lose the habits of camp life when he returned to his former work. On the building site (especially when the supervisor made his tour of inspection) the foreman encouraged us to work faster by shouting: "Action! Action!" I told my friend, "One day you will be back in the operating room, performing a big abdominal operation. Suddenly an orderly will rush in announcing the arrival of the senior surgeon by shouting, 'Action! Action!' " [5]

2. *No one incongruity is viewed the same* by all people. Each person is oriented to the common incongruity in a different way. For instance, it would be difficult for a loving mother to laugh at her alcoholic son's "funny" actions. The alcoholic might laugh at himself. His friends might laugh as long as it is not a put-down. But the mother's orientation to the incongruities of her son is too close. Thus what is funny to one may not be to another. Yet the incongruity remains.

Somebody laughing at the incongruities rescues us from a cynical world.

3. If something is funny, *do not try to explain it.* The moment you try to explain it, you will lose the humor.

Jokes cannot be explained and remain funny unless you make a joke out of explaining a joke. But try to explain *that* joke, and the joke is on you! "The correct explanation of a joke not only does not sound funny, but it does not sound like a correct explanation." [6] In order to explain a thing you have to take it seriously; in order to feel humor you have to be playful.

Humor reacts to incongruities. Humor leaves when the incongruities are seen in the raw—when they are intellectualized. But humor comes again through the next laugh, when we are again surprised by our glimpse of the "gap." When humor is evaluated, it no longer is funny. On the other hand, a totally serious self is dealing with, of all things, the subject of humor.

In his lecture at our church Muggeridge said, "Sometimes I would hear from a reader, usually a clergyman, 'I don't understand the joke on page seven.' " Muggeridge said, "I would painfully try to explain. Then he would write back, 'Now I understand. But it doesn't make me laugh.' "

4. There is *no humor about God,* love, faith, hope, prayer, the sacraments, the cross, the call to preach, the sacred. Some subjects are too serious to laugh at, namely, God, love, faith, etc. These experiences lie within the framework of Truth-itself. Ontologically, Truth cannot be laughed at since Truth is the congruous quality that elicits incongruities.[7]

The incongruities show up when we act like we are God; when our act of agape love looks more like eros (in *Christian love,* it is easier to say "I love you" to the Miss America type than to the Phyllis Diller type); when we proclaim a faith that moves mountains, and will not pick up our clothes around the house; when we *hope* for better government, but will not vote; when we pray for God to help us, but will not worship Him in His Church; when we "bear our cross," and make ourselves unbearable for others; when we boast of our call to preach, but say little or nothing about the call to study for the sermon.

5. Since God's Truth makes humor possible, *that insight is divine revelation.* Seeing the logic of humor as divine revelation (and knowing in your heart that it is so) makes you responsive to the Grace that makes the humor possible. This awareness keeps you from being defensive at the sight of your own incongruities. Your awareness that God's Truth reveals every incongruity, however small, alerts you to make sure your humor is accepted as a gesture of good will, rather than ill will. For instance, when you know people who are sensitive, whose feelings are easily hurt, any humor about them is a gamble and should not be tried. However, your good humor with them about yourself can be helpful to those persons. Possibly, humor about something else will alert the easily-offended persons to their own hypersensitive feelings. And they will by vicarious identification accept that humorous "criticism" for themselves. In all situations humor is at work. The God whose Truth provides it also supervises its use. Truth supervises humor's use even after you have used it, and failed to read the signs—after it has backfired on you. God's Grace at that point advises and supervises reconciliation. Finally, all humor, both that which fails and succeeds, needs redemption. It needs more than our attempts at good humor. It needs a sense of forgiveness. There is no humor in that experience. If it is real, forgiveness is absolutely congruous (our sin meets God's Grace). And there is no humor in that.

B. God is not funny; we are. *God laughs at and with us!* "He who sits in the heavens laughs." [8] And God invites the preacher through Truth-illumined incongruities to laugh with Him. It is commonly accepted that a preacher can use a sense of humor.

> So it is a mistake for a preacher to subject the congregation to a long face. There are times of great solemnity in a church; there must be sermons that will not make anybody happy. Duty, repentance, and caring about

those who suffer must be earnestly presented. But if the prevailing mood of the sermon is somber, it is a denial of the Holy Spirit and a travesty on Christianity. A sour minister is a heretic of the worst sort. "These things have I spoken to you, that my joy may be in you, and that your joy may be full," was Jesus' promise. The prodigal's father in the parable represents God the Father when he says, "Let us make merry." That is still His invitation. When we come to church there is much for us to make merry about. *Sursum corda*—"Lift up your hearts!"—is the ancient invitation. So the minister does not have to be too embarrassed if something he says makes people laugh right out in church.[9]

A few preachers are criticized—chiefly by other preachers—for relying too heavily on humor. There have been few great speakers or writers, lay or clerical, who have scorned its use. By its use one can produce effects that can be secured in no other way. Yet the preacher who handles humor effectively is a rarity; large numbers of his colleagues either avoid it altogether or present it with extreme ineptness.[10]

Whether a preacher uses humor or not, he needs to be in good humor. And that includes the ability to laugh. Uncle Remus showed the children that Brer Rabbit had a Laughing Place. Preachers need a Laughing Place in their lives. And they need to share that "Place" with others—in life, if not in sermons.

At the outset, let it be said that you do not have to have a keen sense of humor to be an acceptable preacher. Some of the best have preached in a totally serious manner. But it should also be admitted that these absolutely serious preachers might have been stronger preachers if they had opened their eyes to the incongruities about them. That staid

10

sort has furnished many an audience unintended humor, which affords the best laughs of all. For instance, there was an elderly bishop known for his dignified, staid, *straight* piety. He could not find wrong in people even when they told him. Those closest to him tried to shield his clean mind against the dirt of the world. To them he was too good a man; they wanted to see him protected against any evil contamination. One day he asked his secretary to order for him an issue of *Playboy Magazine*. He wanted to read for himself the *Playboy* philosophy, and preach a sermon that spoke to that mentality. When the magazine arrived, his secretary unwrapped the magazine and gave it to the bishop, with those pages stapled together that she felt too offensive for his innocent eyes! He never saw the centerfold!

He told this story *straight*. He seemed pleased that his secretary had thus protected him. The audience erupted with riotous laughter. The bishop never seemed to know what caused the humor. Neither did he seem to care. He continued preaching his *straight* dead-serious sermon. Such *straight* preaching furnishes moments of hilarious unintended humor. If that were intended humor, he would have won an Oscar for his acting.

Some people are born with a greater sense of humor than others. Spontaneously, they seem to pick up incongruities and see funny things that pass others by. Some do not seem to be able to sense the incongruities. This writer contends that these persons can, with effort, learn to see the humor that is effortlessly witnessed by some. *Straight,* serious-talking preachers can know the Truth, and that frees them to see incongruities.

C. *God saves the preacher through good humor.*

1. *Good humor saves the preacher from cynicism.* Some people will not see incongruities. Others may see the incongruities, but their own negative attitudes interpret the incongruities cynically. Their conclusion is: "If the world is incongruous, why bother?"

The cynical preacher sinks into a disparaging use of humor. He expresses the incongruities he sees in hurtful humor.

> Laughter that grows out of disparagement, and at the same time fosters feelings of superiority, may be strongly anti-Christian in its effects. There are sadistic, vindictive elements in many forms of humor. William L. Stidger says of a fictional friend, mouthpiece for many of his humorous stories: "Conrad has no racial prejudice, but he enjoys racial humor." Psychological studies indicate that such a judgment is sheer nonsense, wishful thinking adorned with a halo.[11]

A preacher is called to interpret incongruities in faith. "Faith in truth gives true Faith and frees one to have a sense of humor." [12] Faith accepts the incongruities, and moves beyond them to God. Faith knows things that unfaith does not know. Faith chuckles in an up-tight world. To illustrate: The aging process is an agonizing ordeal for many. For some, growing old is synonymous with death. Not so with the late Methodist Bishop Herbert Welsh who died at the age of 107. Dr. Ralph Sockman once recalled how Bishop Welsh, toward the end of his life, got to complaining about some things. He said in his early days he had been a missionary, and just after he left the mission field they raised the salary of missionaries. He then was elected a Bishop, and the year after he retired they raised the salary of bishops. "Now the girls are wearing mini-skirts and I'm going blind," he concluded.

Such humor is seen as a vital expression of sincere faith.

2. *Good humor saves the preacher from silliness.* Since the ludicrous involves perception of an absurdity, it excludes foolishness, pure silliness, senselessness. The ludicrous encounter must yield not to blindness, but to an insight.[13]

The preacher who acts cute could use a sense of humor. Once he sees with the help of Truth that he was acting more foolish than funny, he might then poke fun at himself for thinking he was funny. And that would be good humor. The preacher who swaggers to the pulpit and tries to make a joke out of everything has not seen the Truth. In the following case the preacher got so ridiculous with his attempt to be funny that he lost the audience. From the pulpit he said to the congregation, "Say, 'Amen!' "

The congregation said, "Amen."

He said, "Say, 'Amen,' again."

They said, "Amen," again.

He said, "Some of you said, 'Amen, again.' "

He said, "Say, 'So.' "

Some of them said, "So."

He then informed them they had fulfilled the scripture Psalm 107:2: "Let the redeemed of the Lord say *so.*"

Some in the congregation groaned. A few tried to laugh. The message turned out to be a fair interpretation of an acceptable thesis. But that bit of victory was in spite of the display of cuteness.

How can someone have a sense of humor who thinks he already has it, but doesn't (and likely thinks nobody else does!)? He cannot, unless he is open to change. Without openness, the poor deluded "comic" will go through life patting himself on the back for being funny, and others will be laughing at him because he thought he was and wasn't!

> As the crackling of thorns under a pot, so is the laughter of fools.[14]

3. *Good humor saves the preacher from superiority.* The preacher's vocation calls for him to be an assertive person. This can come across to others as authority or power.

What young minister has wholly escaped the temptation? The people praise him for the qualities of his sermons, and for the hope they see in them. It feeds his vanity and he soon grows restless without applause. The love of praise soon passes into a love of power. And then, farewell to the simplicity and openness of his spirit! There is no longer the lowly mind of his Master. He becomes a church manager and politician. He is dogmatic in his preaching and conversation, brooking no opposition to his plans, intolerant of differences of opinion.[15]

That sense of autonomous power in the preacher can be broken by a sense of humor at himself. When he sees how ridiculous he is acting in relation to how he ought to be and laughs at himself, his overpowering assertion turns to an authority of the spirit—an authority that people respect in the preacher. This esteemed authority is not felt by the preacher so much as it is recognized by the people. He may take it on faith that he has that God-given authority when he can laugh at himself for thinking he had power. His assertion now is not: "Look at me; listen to me; do as I say." His assertion through laughter at himself is: "Here I am. If God can love me, He can love anybody!" This is asserting yourself for God's sake.

When a preacher is willing to laugh at himself, he strengthens his credibility with the audience, and actually gains authority from them. An audience enjoys the put-down of authority. The gap in an authority figure is wider than in an ordinary person. The humor is more easily seen. The put-down is much funnier when it happens to a bishop than when it happens to a student pastor.

A well-known Methodist bishop, starting out on a speaking tour, delivered his initial address to the men's club of a large church. He told several fresh, sparkling anecdotes. But because he wished to repeat them at other meetings, he requested reporters not to include any of them in their accounts.

A cub reporter turned in a glowing report of the occasion. He gave a concise summary of the address, then concluded: "The bishop also told a number of good stories that cannot be published." [16]

When a preacher is caught in a moment of unintended humor, if he can laugh at himself, his credibility goes up in the mind of the audience. A bishop in an annual conference was preaching. While he preached, one saintly lady laced his sermon together with a high-toned hearty "Amen!" At one point in his sermon he said, "I don't pretend to be the best preacher in the world—" Before he could say another word, that little lady's strong "Amen!" broke up the audience. The beauty of that event came when the bishop led in the laughter at himself.

When you can laugh at yourself, you will not take advantage of your authority and act in a manner that will cause your audience to lose their respect for you. When you laugh with them at yourself, your authority is strengthened.

4. God saves the preacher through humor. First, the preacher must realize he is the chief of sinners.

The High Priest, in Old Testament days, knew that he was under the judgment of God. When he went into the Holy of Holies on the Day of Atonement, he confessed his own sins as he proceeded to confess for all the people. "All men have sinned and fallen short of the glory of God." Today as then, "all men" is a phrase which includes the minister.

The best he can be is a redeemed sinner. It is only through the minister's recognition of this need for for-

15

giveness and divine assistance that he is compassionate enough to lead the people.[17]

The look at one's own inconsistencies alone reveals that something is wrong. That *something* is sin. When the preacher sees his pride acting like what he is not, he sees himself the sinner. He may also laugh at his stupidities. A sinner who can laugh at his own foibles is a ready candidate for forgiveness. A preacher can preach about this forgiveness only when he knows the experience. He can also reveal bumblings and stumblings through a laugh at himself. And the people will love him for it.

The audience will know that the preacher has been saved from his sin when they see in him the ability to laugh at himself. That sense of humor indicates he has seen himself as "unacceptable." He is split. He is not who he ought to be, but he knows that God loves him anyway. Thus he has accepted the unacceptable in himself. And he laughs.

As he laughs at himself, he can help others laugh at themselves. Dr. Gerald McCulloch, professor at Garrett Seminary, received a paper from a student that read: "Jesus has taken my quilt away." In the margin of his paper Dr. McCulloch wrote: "That's all right. He will send His Comforter." That sense of humor is God's salvation at work.

5. "A merry heart doeth good like a medicine: but a broken spirit drieth the bones." [18]

Humor saves the preacher from negative attitudes. It offers a power-of-positive-thinking dimension that is God-centered. In every incongruity there are the positive and negative dimensions. You *are not* who you think you are (i.e., the ill-prepared preacher who bluffs his way through the sermon). That is the incongruity known through humor. The experience of Truth carries a sense of "oughtness" with it. While it shows the incongruity, it shows that you "ought" not misuse that insight. While it reveals the incongruity, it nudges you to

16

follow the positive use of that insight. The incongruity closes when you become who you ought to be. That "oughtness" is God's power of positive thinking that closes the gap.

This power closes the gap in a positive direction, in a direction that affirms the well-being of the persons toward whom the humor is directed, whether at you or somebody else. A laugh at yourself builds you up. The ability to laugh at yourself is a power of positive thinking.

Phillips Brooks says:

> The first business of the preacher is to conquer the tyranny of his moods, and to be always ready for his work. Any mood which makes us unfit to preach at all, or really weakens our will to preach, is bad. Then is the time for the conscience to bestir itself and for the man to be a man. It was not good that the minister should be worshipped and made an oracle. It is still worse that he should be flattered and made a pet. Never appeal for sympathy.[19]

You cannot appeal for sympathy and laugh at yourself at the same time. Self-indulgence and self-humor do not mix. A willingness to laugh at your own foibles will include a laugh at your own self-pity. You cannot pick and choose what you are willing to laugh at in yourself. That process reveals you are still taking yourself seriously because you are attempting to rule in or out what is laughable in your life. A true laugh at yourself comes when you lay yourself open to Truth, and take whatever incongruity comes up, including self-pity. When in a bad mood, acknowledge a stupidity you pulled recently. Laugh. And then go about your business.

When somebody becomes uncooperative, when the pressures of the job begin to press on me, when an unpleasantness hounds me, and self-pity starts eating at me, I have something that helps me get turned around. Before I leave the house, I take off an imaginary hat and "throw" it outside. This ludicrous acting-out is seen by me, my wife, and the Good Lord. We all laugh and I go out into a world that never throws my "hat" back.

Divine Power interprets the incongruity in a positive manner. This can be illustrated in the story about the downcast fellow who cried, "Why me? Why me?"

About that time a deep bass voice came from above: "Because there's just something about you that bugs me to death!"

In this case, it was expected that the cry of self-pity would be rewarded with pity. But the unexpected was what occurred. Deep down inside, we probably know we do bug people to death. If that story were interpreted as a totally serious view of how God sees us, that is negative thinking. When that story is used to shake us to an awareness that God accepts us, "bugs" and all, that is positive thinking.

A preacher possessed by hope is prone to be positive in the use of humor. If he hopes for a better life for everybody (not just a select few), he will use humor in a way that points in that direction. This hope must be expressed at a level deeper than words. A hypercritical attitude can mouth hope without knowing hope. A preacher who uses humor must know hope, talk hopefully, act hopefully, *be* hopeful. That hope is the springboard for humor. Without that hope the preacher's efforts at humor will too often fall flat. With hope his humor will not hurt, but will help. It will not destroy, but will redeem.

If love does not prevail between you and your audience, do not joke with them. If there is "bad blood" between you and your audience, your joke will be a "dig," the power of negative thinking. "God is love." [20] Love makes you sensitive to the people to whom you speak. Love helps you see the humor, helps you know when not to use humor, and when to use it. "Love never fails." [21]

6. A sense of humor, committed to the Truth that makes humor possible, *saves the preacher from the insatiable craving for sensationalism.*

The evil of sensationalism is in the undue expression of the man; it puts the man before the message. It has been wittily said that the difference between an advertiser and a sensational preacher was that the first advertised his wares and the second advertised himself. It may fill the church and trumpet the preacher's name by the lips of thousands, but that may not work for righteousness and establish the kingdom of spiritual life. You may lose your fortune and gain another; you may lose your wife and win another; but if you lose your soul. "Good-by, John," was the way a certain noted preacher of our day tried to express the value of the soul. A flippant sensationalism can only deaden the true hunger of the soul, dissipate earnest thought by its irreverence, and in the end prove a feeble rival to the comic opera and the variety theatre.[22]

"The Johnny Carson Show" sounds right for Johnny Carson. He thrives on sensationalism, and rightly so. But hardly would we be comfortable with "The Mother Teresa Show."

When you can see your own incongruities and inconsistencies, and can laugh at your own inadequacies, there is less likelihood that you will make the play for sensationalism.

The very act of laughing at yourself conquers selfishness at that time. You are "split apart" in this glance at yourself, and for the time captured by Truth. Selfishness works when the self is in charge, and cannot function when God is in charge. In good humor God's Truth always predominates.

A sense of humor reveals a sympathetic nature not expressed by the dead-serious person. Somber sympathy shown by the serious-only minded shrouds a person. Sympathy from one with a sense of humor includes the warm hand-shake, the pat on the back, and the twinkle in the eye with or without the tear. And lifts the spirit.

A preacher with a sense of humor expresses a hope that eludes the dead-serious. The dead-serious always look and talk hopelessly.

Some of the dead-serious try to show they are spiritually wise. This foolish effort is not attempted by the preacher with a sense of humor. Stop now and think of the preacher who thinks he alone is God's gift of wisdom to the world. What he thought was courage looks like conceit. And he knows more about nothing than anybody.

A sense of humor rescues the preacher from the closed mind. By its very nature, a mind that senses *in*congruities cannot be *closed.* A serious-only minded person is not necessarily close-minded. But there is no obvious indication that he is not close-minded. A good-humored preacher leaves no doubt that his mind is open.

You pass the test of humility when you laugh at yourself. When you cannot laugh at your foibles, you *act* humble. When you can laugh at yourself, you *are* humble. There is no greater humbling experience than to be caught by yourself in some foolish act that you knew that you, of all people, would never commit. For instance, I abhor people talking about people—gossipers. And then I realized one day I was the world's worst in talking about those people who talked about people. That self-realization given to me by God's Truth was a humbling experience. Rather than condemning myself—as I had others—I laughed at myself and them! Self-humor conquers vanity, self-pity, and dogmatism.

A laugh at yourself signals that you have been caught by God's Truth, that you have been humbled, and more than that: you now accept yourself as God accepts you. This sense of self-acceptance, accepting the *unacceptable,* gives a deep sense of well-being. At this point you might well be warned: be sure you are not merely acting like you are laughing at yourself in order to win approval. That puts you farther from real self-awareness than the dead-serious. Now you are playing with Truth, and God does not permit that. Truth remains in charge of us. Our surrender to Truth brings an awareness of our foibles. It brings us through self-humor, and keeps us secure. Because God accepts us *in spite of* our foibles, we do too.

D. What has been said about humor in the preacher can be seen in the comparisons and contrasts between *the comic and the good-humored preacher*. Normally you think of a humorist as a stand-up comic. You would not think of a preacher as a humorist because you know a preacher proclaims the Truths of God. Anyone who has been struck by Truth knows there is nothing funny *about* Truth. But look deeper and you will see God's Truth making good humor possible and showing when humor is bad. God's Truth spotlights the incongruities of man. How could you know they were incongruities without Truth telling you? That insight elicits the humor in your mind. A stand-up comic and a preacher may see the same incongruity. Both laugh. But the preacher goes deeper, and sees the overall congruity of God's Truth making nonsense sensible, making humor a valuable asset to man's existence. For instance, the comic and the preacher see the incongruity of the politician who denies he was bribed and says, "I took the money because I did not want to offend my constituency." The comic in his routine quotes the politician, and adds in sarcasm, "Of course he did!" And then he goes on with his jokes. The preacher quotes the politician and says too, "Of course he did." But he does not go on with jokes. He goes deeper by adding something like, "God knows what he did, of course!" The comic uses humor for humor's sake; the preacher uses humor for God's sake.

While the humorist as such *knows about* the religious attitude, he lacks the decisive commitment to it which

21

bespeaks the inwardness of faith. Yet because he had known reflectively the suffering, the moral conflict, and deep disappointments of life, existence has lost its authority over him; in contemplating its pretenses and pathos, the posturing of the finite in the face of the infinite, he grasps the abysmal absurdity of the spectacle.[23]

The comic does not proclaim the truth. When he does, he becomes a preacher.

One of the reasons we get more pleasure from satire than from a sermon, even when the satire is making exactly the same point as the sermon, is that we have an uncomfortable feeling that the minister expects us to do something about it. We enjoy the satire because we know that nobody really expects us to do anything about it, and that we have no real intention of ever doing anything about it. It may not be a moral reaction, but for most human beings it *is* the reaction.[24]

He can be a comic so long as he spells out the absurdities of the incongruities he sees and tries to make nothing out of them. For this reason, the stand-up comic is the only professional who, while doing his thing, does not necessarily reveal the incongruities of his own life. His job is to entertain. He may take as the continuing theme of his act the "nobody appreciates me" routine. You will only know if he really feels that way when he steps off the stage into his real life. This writer on two occasions had the opportunity to talk privately with Bob Hope. In no sense was he the comic in those instances. He was dead-serious, and intensely observant. When he walked on stage, the comic came out. You can see incongruities in the performance of the comic. You see with him the incongruities of others. Even when he makes fun of himself, it takes place in the "others" category of your mind.

The preacher proclaims the Truth. He may or may not use humor in the process. His primary function is to proclaim, not to entertain. But this does not mean that he cannot be entertaining in the process—if the situation lends itself to the use of humor to illustrate a point, or for a special effect to gain or keep attention (this will be discussed in Part VI). This proclamation/entertainment balance must always be kept in the forefront of the preacher's mind.

Some preachers go to excessive lengths in maintaining a stern countenance as they preach. I remember when that mind-set was my *modus operandi*. I was preaching hard when I came to a comment about hell. I paused and said, "This is going to be shocking." A three-year-old from the back piped up at that moment and repeated loud enough for the audience to hear, "This is going to be shocking." The audience laughed. I countered with: "This is not funny!" But it was funny, and my unfunny comment made it funnier than ever.

Have you ever watched children play church? The one who does the preaching inevitably mimics the long-faced parson who never allows a laugh in church. "Stop that laughing!" he yells at one of his less attentive hearers, just as the grown-ups do. And then they all break off in hilarious laughter as they go into some other entertainment. As we have seen, some of the funniest preachers are those who do not intend to be funny at all!

Now let us go to the other extreme. There are some preachers who try to play the stand-up comic on and off the stage. They think they are very funny, and they want everyone to recognize their exceptional sense of humor. You make a serious statement, and they try to turn it into a joke.

"How are you doing today?" you ask.

He answers, "I'm doing it by walking."

You say, "Well, I've missed seeing you around."

He says, "Don't say 'round.' I've gained twenty pounds."

You say, "I'm sorry. I did not mean to offend you."

He says, "No, you are not a sorry fellow. I really like you." Turn that mentality loose in the pulpit and it is "ahgggh!" for the audience.

Somewhere between these two extremes is a meeting ground. You are on that turf when you realize that you are called to proclaim, not entertain. But you may proclaim in a manner pleasant to the ear, and piercing to the heart. Humor does that.

E. *The preacher* includes humor but *goes beyond humor to God.*

1. For humor to have a better opportunity to work for you in a sermon, you must first believe that God's Truth shines over all of life and will show you the incongruities that make for humor, and that humor in its process is divine revelation. *You see with God's Truth everything,* including a look at how humor works in your life. He shows you that you can never laugh *at* Him. Only a sick mind can imagine incongruities in God's nature. God is Love. And you do not laugh at Love. God is Truth. And you do not laugh. at Truth. God is Kind. And you do not laugh at Kindness. God is Good. And you never laugh at Goodness. You never laugh *at* God, but *with* Him you can laugh at all things, including yourself.

You cannot laugh at God's Love. But you can laugh at how you act when you put on the act of Love. If God's Love were as gross as some people act, He would be a fool. He is not. They are. You cannot laugh at Truth, but you can laugh at the manner in which you portray Truth. "I will never tell you a lie," said President Washington. But he probably did once or twice. You cannot laugh at God's Kindness. But you can laugh at the manner in which you portray it. Maybe you keep the Golden Rule in this manner: "I'll be kind to others if others will be kind to me. If they are not kind to me, then I won't be kind to them anymore!" You cannot laugh at God's

Goodness. But you can laugh at how you act good for the wrong reasons: to please somebody, to impress somebody, to compensate for a wrong committed, etc. The ability to laugh at yourself is a must if you ever use humor in your sermons.

This ability to laugh at yourself does not come by trying to be funny, by testing out your sense of humor on all you meet. Rather it comes by knowing who you are in relation to God. Some preachers act like they are above the messages they preach. And they are unintentionally funny in the effort. You can preach forgiveness only after you have been forgiven. I saw this dramatically take place in a preacher's life after he wrote this letter to a fellow minister:

(To protect anonymity names, places, and some events are omitted; dates and numbers are changed)

> Dear_____:
> I have been wrestling with a sermon for weeks that you helped me to start. Today I am hung up and led to write you. For eighteen years I have held a grudge against you. What motivates this you have a right to ask. On a recent Sunday I caught your telecast. At that time I was extremely judgmental of the whole thing. We went to church, and in the quiet time the Lord tore me up. During the silent period my conscience began to condemn me for being so judgmental. I confessed my prejudice, my grudge, and really wished I had not been so picky. Who was I to judge a fellow minister whom God had called?
> - - - - - - -
> - - - - - - -
> For eighteen years I have held this unholy grudge against you. And I want to be rid of it.
> - - - - - -
> I am wrestling with a sermon. The sermon I am wrestling with deals with the idea, "Lord, Help Me to Want

to Forgive as You Forgive." And I do not believe that the Lord is going to let me write it until this letter is complete. And so I am simply asking your forgiveness for my attitude, and resultant actions toward you across the last eighteen years.

- - - - - -
- - - - - -

Perhaps someday we will be thrown together in a way that we can be friends! Perhaps we will not. But in the future I am going to try to be more understanding of who you are and where you come from because I can now accept Whose you are. I pray that the Lord who called us both will continue to bless your ministry.

Cordially,

- - - - - -

P.S. Well, the sermon is now written. How good it is I do not know. But the writing of it sure did flow easily after I wrote the first draft of this letter.

The minister who wrote this letter then went to church and preached the sermon. On the following Monday morning he had not yet mailed the letter. At the bottom of it he penned these words with an exciting flourish of ink: "Monday—It preached good!"

As you read this letter, you can sense the dramatic change and the good humor that forgiveness brought him.

The thing that amazed me about this minister was the after-effects of his forgiveness. A well-balanced, non-judgmental, gentle humor crept into his preaching. He *became* a preacher of good humor.

A preacher who sees man's depressed condition in his own life has the opportunity to use humor for good. His humor allows God's Truth to reveal incongruities in Love, in a caring manner. Humor expressed out of depravity alone (without God) is sick humor.

Bad humor comes when incongruities are imagined wholly within the frame of non-being. Such fantasy incongruities are untruthful, therefore non-essential—no matter how "positive" sounding one spells out the gap of a situation. There is no gap without truth to elicit it. To illustrate: Nazis experienced sick laughter as they fed humans to the ovens. They imagined the Jews were inferior to how the Jews acted, *no matter how they acted.* There was no good act because there was no good Jew. That viewpoint provided the basis for an imagined glimpse of the incongruity whenever they saw a learned Jew suffering. They thought it was funny. When incongruities are fantasized with non-being, it is bad humor, because there are no incongruities in non-being. Ontologically speaking, then, bad humor finally is not humor at all.[25]

A preacher who knows he is capable of sick humor is less likely to practice it. He is more likely to laugh at his own incongruities.

Forgiveness is essential for you if you are to practice using humor divinely blessed. That experience takes away any vindictiveness that could ease into your humor and hurt somebody. Sin destroys good humor, and hurts people in the process. I once knew a preacher who had a finely tuned sense of humor. He laughed a lot and made others laugh. They enjoyed his company. Then he committed sins that hurt his family and friends. He still laughs. His friends try to laugh. Their faces look like they are laughing. But theirs are hollow laughs. Only forgiveness of sin can restore his good humor, can restore a truthful integrity to his life. You cannot plan to have a sense of humor, and have one, if you leave God out of your plans.

2. *Take God seriously, and yourself less seriously.* This trust of God's Truth is faith. This faith in God permits you to

hang loose and laugh at your own incongruities. People look at you and say, "He surely does have self-confidence, or he would not pull that off." And that is what they must say in order to accept your humor. A retiring and subdued person never gets across a funny story. But what you must know, as a preacher, is this: Your confidence does not come from self, but from God, whom you trust far more than you trust yourself. A laugh with God at yourself gives you credibility (ethos) with your audience (more on this in Part VI).

When you preach faith in God, when you live your faith in God, you will better know how to use humor. Because the humor you see is God-centered, not self-centered. Self-centered humor produces sick humor; God-centered humor produces redemptive humor—a humor that makes life worthwhile in spite of its tragic dimensions. Self-centered humor originates in depravity and produces depraved laughter. This was the laughter of the Philistines who mocked blind Samson, and ridiculed him for their own pleasure. God's humor was there too, but they were too self-centered to see it. In an un-self-conscious manner Samson "saw" the humor. We see his practicing this humor when he said to the lad at his side, "Would you find a post I can *lean* against for a rest?" Samson leaned against the column and *rested* so hard that it caved in under his *restful* weight! And then he looked with God at the crowd. He saw them laugh themselves literally *to death!*

Your faith works for you as you permit Truth to shut down the urge to justify your every failure. I have seen preachers try to use humor to cover their mistakes. That effort to use humor as a means of self-justification may evoke laughter from those who feel sorry for you and want to help you cover your error. But there remain those others who drop their heads in embarrassment for you. When they do that, your credibility is affected. I remember the time a preacher stumbled and fell before a gathering crowd. He picked himself up and ran as if a bee had stung him. Later when he started to speak, he spent some time trying to explain that he had to hurry and get something from his car. He tried to joke about it. It all fell flat. Everybody knew that he had made an unplanned flight of embarrassment. He took himself too seriously.

A preacher was being introduced to an audience who already knew him. (There is latent danger in that situation!) The introducer said, "Our speaker has been honored for his achievements. Maybe he will tell you about the honor he has received."

The speaker came to the rostrum and said, "Which one?" He used the introducer's remarks to put himself *up*. There was a ripple of nervous laughter at his comment—that showed his self-centeredness. A preacher who takes himself too seriously cannot trust himself with humor. His problem is that he thinks he is humorous! And he falls on his face in his effort to be so. A preacher who looks through the family album and laughs at those funny-looking people, but who looks in the mirror and never cracks a smile, will not be able to handle humor. He is too self-centered.

The preacher's faith in God is what speaks to his audience. They see his faith when they see that he is courageous enough to accept his own incongruities and laugh at his own inadequacies. Others are going to laugh at you anyway (remember, everybody, including you, has incongruities). It is a witness of your faith if they can see courage in you as you laugh with them at yourself.

You may see the joke without having faith in God. But you will not see the humor without God's Truth. That Truth is available to everybody. Not everybody gives God credit for Truth. When you give God credit, when you have faith in God, you will not make those you joke about into a joke. You will joke with a sense of reverence for those about whom you joke.

3. As a Christian, *you can joke with others only if you love them.* If you do not love them, do not try joking about them. Your joking backfires because your ridicule arises out of disdain. This is a congruity of negative attitudes toward those about whom you joke. Without an incongruity seen by the audience, their half-hearted laughter means: "I can't believe he said that!" The audience must know you speak out of love for the ones you joke about. When you love, your jokes turn on a positive interpretation of the incongruity. You can joke about a good singer by saying, "I offered to give him some free singing lessons" (this can be used if *you,* the speaker, are *not* a good singer). That humor causes a laugh and builds up the one joked about.

That love of God in you gives you protection against misuse of humor. You choose not to joke about somebody being tongue-tied if that person is tongue-tied. It would hurt him. Your intention is not to hurt, but in playful humor to help. You may joke about someone being tongue-tied if that person is anything but tongue-tied! You can if he is a silver-tongued orator. That humor enhances the one joked about.

Or the humor *could* enhance those toward whom the humor is directed if they would let it—if they would see the Truth, and change toward the positive side of the incongruity spotted by Truth in their lives. Jesus said to the self-righteous Pharisees, "You have such a fine way of rejecting the commandments of God." [26] You, too, could use these same words if you were talking to an audience of modern-day "Pharisees." You could use these words if you were not a "Pharisee" when you said them—if you were not self-righteous in your comment. You can say just about anything in humor that you want to if you love. If you love, you will want only to say what will help.

With God's love you are less likely to offend when you use humor. The humor of the dying parishioner I visited in the hospital was beautiful because he loved his pastor. He was in his last hours on this earth. His wife and children were by the bedside. The man was so sick that he did not feel like opening his eyes. He knew I had come into the room. The nurse entered the room with two capsules large enough to choke a horse. Someone quietly said, "Those are the biggest capsules I ever saw." Without opening his eyes the dying man said, "Give 'em to the preacher!"

That day the man died, but not his sense of humor. I reminded the congregation at the funeral service of that comment. Their subdued laughter through tears revealed God's love had reached them through the humor of one loved. God's love made his joke right for him to say, for me to repeat, and for the friends to enjoy. Humor in love redeems.

F. *The ultimate example of good humor comes through Jesus Christ.*

At the tomb of Lazarus the humanity of Jesus was so close to the tragic death that He wept. With His mind He knew the incongruities of this existence; but at that particular moment He saw no humor.

Jesus carried His cross. They hung Him on that cross. He carried the weight of the world's sin. He was too close to man's tragic existence to see humor.

But the humorous surrounds the cross. We can see the tragedy which surrounds the cross in the lives of those who had the power. They hung Christ on the cross to restore peace and order! They put Him out of the way because He was not religious! Not good enough! They had a fine way of rejecting the commandments of God. Tragic man may laugh at Christ off or on the cross. But the last laugh is on the one who tries it. They tried it by putting on him the crown of thorns, the purple robe, and the mocking title "King of the Jews" on a sign over his head. And they laughed at him. But

31

their mockery backfired when their protected order was smashed by those who used their same reasoning—the Jews had to be conquered to maintain peace and order. Then Romans ruled the world ruthlessly in maintaining *their* definition of peace and order. And then the Roman-protected order was smashed by those who used the same reasoning—*that* order had to be conquered to maintain peace and order. Thusly, the human tragedy becomes compounded. And so do the ironies of human actions—we miss our greatness when we act great and powerful! It is to our credit—a sign of our self-transcendence, our finite greatness—when we laugh with Christ at the tragic in ourselves and others who throughout time stand around the cross of Christ.[27]

While Jesus was man, He also was Truth. "I am the way, the truth, and the life." [28] That Truth permitted Jesus to bear His cross. It was the Truth that He, the human, *could* bear the cross, *could* suffer, die, and live again. That same incarnate Truth permitted Jesus, the man, at a *distance* from the tragic to laugh at the incongruities of people.

By self-transcendence we can be removed far enough from these areas to laugh. The humor is not directed at the person in tragedy (though on the surface that looks like the case). It is directed at the tragic aspects of their lives—at *hubris* gone wild—at non-being. Jesus Christ loved people; yet He ridiculed their *hubris:* "You have such a fine way of rejecting the commandments of God." He pointed out their fine way in a ludicrous statement: "You strain at a gnat and swallow a camel." Those toward whom these remarks were directed accepted the tragic as a way of life—they had the power (that proved to be their failure). While participating with this greatness-tragedy ambiguity in their lives Jesus used humor freely—thus permitting in his own humanity the greatness to prevail over the potentially tragic. His own self-transcendence continued throughout his involvement with human tragedy, and humor was a part of it.

Jesus expressed no humor-at-self on the cross because there was no *hubris*-gone-wild in his life to make for any self-humor.[29]

Jesus, the man, laughed at finite incongruities that He as a man might contribute to. But He could not laugh at any sin-caused incongruities in Himself because He knew no sin.

However, *being* the Truth, He picked up fast on pride-initiated incongruities in people, and he laughed whether they did or not.

His major weapon against the Pharisees' self-righteousness was laughter, and he used it fully. He reduced all of them to fools by insisting they too were adulterers in their hearts (Matthew 5:27-28). His strategy of laughter was directed toward all who assume they can solve the problem of sin by rules. Divine judgment laughs at such pretentiousness.

And men too must learn to laugh about what is truly foolish, that which is masquerading as power and disguised as goodness, that which is incongruous from the perspective of faith. This perspective, to see both the faith of one's self and the power of what a man equipped by faith can do, is to live *sub specie aeternitatis,* not by one's own doing, but by the gift of grace.[30]

Following are some of those humorous occasions in the life of Jesus:

Throughout the Gospel Jesus moves on, scarcely touching the ground, yet, somehow, his words as they reach us are resonant with the overtones of irony. Let

him without sin cast the first stone. Ah! It was the overtones that caught the ear, the ear of his audience,
though not always that of the reader, and when the
accused turned to face the speaker they found his finger
not pointed to them in scorn, but tracing pictures in the
sand. Can one not laugh with one's fingers as well as
one's lips?[31]

Following are some samples of Jesus' use of humor:
1. "Is a candle brought to be put under a bushel, or under
a bed?" [32]
Can't you see people *lighting lamps and putting them under
bushels and beds* for all to see by?
"No," you say, "that's absurd."
That is the point. Jesus used the absurd to make his point.
2. Look at the young *women who went to the all-night
party.* They carried their lamps without oil with them wherever they went.[33]
"That's ridiculous!" you say.
That is why Jesus used it. He used the ridiculous to make
his point.
3. Jesus asked the people, *"What did you go out in the
wilderness to behold?*—a reed shaken by the wind? Why then
did you go out? To see a man clothed in soft raiment?" [34]
They guffawed at the idea that anybody would walk for
miles in the wilderness to see a reed blow in the wind, or to
see someone dressed in the soft garments worn by those in
the king's house.
"Of course not!" they would laugh. And then their attention would turn to the real reason for their going into the
wilderness—to see John the Baptist. And then Jesus led them
to see John as the introducer, and Himself as the One introduced.
4. Jesus told *the story of an incompetent servant* discharged
by his master. The servant said, "What shall I do, since my
master is taking away the stewardship from me? I am not

34

strong enough to dig, and I am ashamed to beg." [35] The laborers and beggars who heard this must have broken up with laughter.

5. Jesus scoffed at the *professional religionists* who painted their faces and dressed in a manner that made it *look like* they were fasting [36] and at those who strutted about in pompous attire.[37] He mimicked them as sulking, whining children: "We piped music to you, and you wouldn't dance. We mourned, and you would not lament." [38] He accused them of tooting their own horns to attract attention to their acts of charity.[39] He mocked the prayer of the hard-hearted Pharisee who nearly broke his arm patting himself on the back.[40]

6. We laugh with Jesus at the man who thinks so highly of himself that, when he goes to a banquet, *he heads for the head table.* He knows he belongs there. He sits down. Everyone in the banquet hall observes his pompous posture at the head table. Then the host goes up to the man and says, "I am sorry, but I am going to have to ask you to leave this head table, and go down to the end of the line. Someone more important than you has just arrived."

The defeated egotist had to get up in front of everybody and go to the end of the line. All eyes followed him as he was seated in the darkest corner of the banquet hall. As he walked to the end of the line some piped up all along, "Where you going?" "Did you forget something?" "I *thought* I saw you at the head table." "Going the wrong way, aren't you?" Worse than words were those who just looked at him and grinned. The 100 foot distance turned into 100 miles. It took forever to get to the end of the line.

"How much better it would be," Jesus said, "for the host to come to get you from the end of the line, and take you to the front—all the way to the head table. You could hear the whispers as you walked by: 'I did not know he belonged up there.' '*He* is an honored guest.' 'He must be a very important person.' " [41]

7. Good humor on the part of the preacher can see what

Jesus saw when He pictured a fellow *trying to pick a speck* out of a neighbor's eye without even noticing a log hanging out of his own eye![42]

8. *Jesus gave the excuses of the men* who would not be able to come to the great supper. The first said, "I have bought a piece of ground, and I must go see it." He had seen it a dozen times before he bought it, a dozen times after he had bought it. But, of course, at this particular time he *had* to go. It was an emergency. Another said, "I have bought a fine yoke of oxen, and I need to go test them out." He had tested them a dozen times before he bought them, a dozen times after he had bought them. But, of course, at this particular time he *had* to go. It was an emergency. Another said, "Oh, I would just love to come, but I have married a wife, and cannot come." [43] That could have been a legitimate excuse. She would not let him!

9. When Jesus said, "Neither cast ye your *pearls before swine,*" [44] that incongruity pictures the ludicrous to the point of the absurd. Imagine people purchasing expensive pearls and then taking them to the pig pen and throwing them to the pigs. Pigs appreciate pearls about as much as demons appreciate love. In humor Jesus made His point.

10. Jesus said, "It is easier for *a camel* to go *through the eye of a needle* than for a rich man to enter into the kingdom of God." [45] Envision a camel trying to get through the eye of a needle!

11. Jesus said, *"Ye blind guides,* which strain at a gnat, and swallow a camel." [46] Blind *guides?* While straining a gnat out of their soup, they swallow a camel—humps, feet, and all—and never feel it go down!

> Soul and body must live together with a measure of domestic peace, if wisdom is to be the child of their union, and Christ, like Aristotle, never forgot that this transcendental divorce is wrong no matter which party

36

sues for it. Aristotle converted this insight into a system of metaphysics, while Jesus taught the philosophy inherent in laughter.[47]

Jesus has given you an example so that you would be able to do as He has done to you.

Peter talks about the example Christ gives us: "For even hereunto were ye called: because Christ also suffered for us, leaving us an example, that ye should follow his steps." [48]

Scripture calls us to follow Christ's example in every way. And that includes His sense of humor. A sense of humor that comes as our eyes follow the spotlight of His Truth.

We conclude this Part I, concerning humor in the preacher, with this statement: If you accept Truth as the Divine Power that spotlights the incongruities and elicits the humor, that is with you to help you know when in love to speak in good humor the incongruity He has revealed—if you in your heart and mind trust His Truth, you are ready to go on to Part II.

PART II

HUMOR IN
DEVOTIONS

HUMOR IN
DEVOTIONS

Part I has alerted you to your own incongruities. Your devotions, discussed in Part II, can, with practice, help you keep that sense of humor toward yourself. Since God's Truth illumines your incongruities, and you draw closer to God in your devotions, it follows that the closer you get to God, the more Truth illumines your incongruities. Humor should be a by-product of your devotions to God. It is the purpose of Part II to help you see what takes place, whether you know or accept it or not. Accepting the Truth that spotlights your incongruities brings you closer to God. Devotions are meant to do that.

A. *In your devotional Bible study you can see your own incongruities.* We do not like to talk about it, but for many of us Bible reading is difficult. And we are supposed to be the experts. I once preached a Revival for a preacher who asked me, "Where in the Bible is the story about the little boy who was going to prove the old wise man of the hills was not so wise?" (The lad had a live bird in his hands. He was going to ask the old man if the bird were dead or alive. If the old man said "dead," he would release the bird. If the old man said "alive," the boy would kill the bird. When the boy got to the old wise man, he asked: "Is this bird in my hands dead or alive?" The old man said, "As you will, my son.") That is a good story, and it reads like a parable that Jesus told. But it is not in the Bible. That preacher has his daily devotions, but is he reading the Bible, or is he *trying* to read the Bible? Is it a chore?

It can be difficult. Bible reading is not the easiest habit in the world. Oftentimes it is downright aggravating—especially if you cannot pronounce the word, much less know what it means. Abe Lincoln told this story about one of his classmates he had in earlier years:

> All our reading was done from the Bible and we stood up in a long line and read the scriptures aloud. One day our lesson was about the faithful Israelites who were thrown into the fiery furnace and were delivered by the Lord without so much as being scorched. One little fellow had to read the verses in which appeared, for the first time, the names Shadrach, Meshach and Abednego. The boy stumbled on Shadrach, floundered on Meshach and went all to pieces on Abednego. Instantly the hand of the teacher gave him a cuff on the head that left him wailing and blubbering as the next boy in line went on with the reading. By the time the first round was over he had quieted down and stopped sniffling.
>
> His blunder and disgrace were forgotten by the others in the class until it was almost his turn to read again. Suddenly he sent up a wail which alarmed even the teacher, who with rather unusual gentleness asked, "What's the matter now?"
>
> Pointing with a shaking finger at the verse which in a few minutes would fall to him to read, the boy managed to stammer, "Look there, teacher, there comes those same d--- three fellows again." [49]

Bible reading may be difficult, but it does not have to be. Read the Bible as if God were looking over your shoulders pointing out the incongruities of the Bible characters. Dr.

Norman Vincent Peale in his Foreword to my book, *Ontology of Humor*, says about an old friend, H. B. Andrews:

> This may appear to be an odd reaction, for Mr. Andrews' total formal education encompassed only the first three grades of school. But he became one of the leading businessmen of Syracuse, New York. He was an extraordinary man. He invented the dishwasher, operated the first supermarket in the United States, and had a wide reputation as a wise and perceptive layman. He was truly a self-made scholar—a man of learning.
>
> He explained his "wisdom" and in-depth insights into the reality of existence simply by saying that he "went to school to the Bible, the greatest university and library of books."
>
> He would not have been familiar with the professional terminology used in this book, but with his keen mind and spiritually sharpened mental perceptiveness, Mr. Andrews profoundly comprehended the nature of existence or being. To him all being was spiritually conceived, all existence designed with perfection, since it was created by God, the Perfect Being. Yet he saw and genuinely appreciated the incongruities in human existence. "God cannot be understood without recognizing his sense of humor," he would say. His Bible was interlined with his own characteristic comments. "Ha Ha," he would write on the margin where a sinner was described as experiencing his just desserts. "Ha Ha," said Brother Andrews (as he was called), "this fellow got what was coming to him." [50]

I enjoy telling Old Testament stories in my sermons. For years I preached to a Sunday School teacher who sat straight as a board, still as a mouse, and stern as a stone. The more the congregation laughed at the stories, the more straight, still, and stern she sat. She enjoyed those stories about as much as a Democrat enjoys stories told by a Republican. Finally one day she came down after the service and "complimented" a sermon. I loved the way she said it. She shook my hand and was turning away as she said, "I like your New Testament preaching about Jesus. But stay away from that Old Testament. I don't like those Old Testament stories."

I tried to explain that these stories in the Old Testament were the stories Jesus read and talked about. I do not believe she heard me. There was no indication from the back of her head that she did.

Now there is something for you to think about. If those Old Testament scriptures were adequate for the Son of God, but not for you, then that puts you above the Son of God in your thinking. And anybody who feels he knows more about the Bible than the Son of God will have problems meditating in wonder and awe and praise of God. The whole Bible is God's Word. He speaks to you through the Bible, and that includes the funny parts. With an open mind, the truth of the Bible becomes for you a hearing aid. If you want to hear from God, read your Bible—all of it. And devotions are one time to do this.

Christ has given us much good humor in scriptures. We should follow His example in our devotional reading of scripture, and not purposely romanticize scripture. Often when we "devotionalize" scripture, we romanticize it, and make it fit our rosy picture of how we want it to sound. Read somber tones into some scriptures, and you miss the meaning. You lose the meaning of the conversation of Jesus with the Samaritan woman at Jacob's well when you romanticize it. You "devotionalize" it when you clothe her words in pious tones—when you make her sound like a Christian—when you make every comment of everybody sound "inspirational." One would assume that she was not *that* pure in soul and actions. That is not hard to assume when you consider she had known five husbands, and the man she was living with was not her husband! She was hardly talking to Christ from a high level of spiritual bliss! She would not be sounding "devotional," but instead, like an enemy of the Jew. Her nature and ethnic situation being what it was, she would have indignantly questioned why Jesus, a Jew, would ask a Samaritan for a drink of water. When we read that story under the illumination of Truth, a self-righteous woman speaks with indignant sarcasm: "You don't have a bucket or rope. And the well is deep," implying that any man with common sense ought to know that. This she said to One who had all the sense in the world! Truth reveals the incongruity of the woman acting like what she was not. Humor in devotional Bible reading protects you from making scripture "devotional"—from eisegeting into the scripture your romantic notions.

After sensing with Truth the incongruities of the Bible characters, you would be wise to put yourself in their places because they are the ones with whom you can identify. The trouble with us preachers is that when we read the Bible stories, we tend to identify ourselves with the good guys, the prophets, the apostles, and even Jesus! When we see that the incongruities of the Bible characters are our incongruities, our Bible reading in devotions (and preaching!) takes on a whole new meaning for us. We can laugh at ourselves in the Bible.

In a church there was a layman who sat on one of the back rows in the sanctuary during the worship hour and listened by transistor radio to the preaching of the pastor of First Baptist Church. One of the ushers asked him, "Why do you sit in this church, and listen to another preacher while our preacher is preaching?"

"Because the Baptist preacher can preach," he said.

"Well, why don't you pick up and just go down there to that church and listen to him?" the usher asked.

"They don't have cushions down there," the man said.

B. *The prayer time in our devotions may actually begin with an incongruity.* We know we ought to pray. So we do. But we do not pray as we ought because we act like we are praying when we are not. Our minds and hearts are elsewhere.

The setting for prayer is made once the urgency to pray hits you. That sense of urgency starts the prayer time. You do not start with a prescribed manner. The manner comes naturally when you start where you are in your experience. At a given prayer time maybe you do not have much to say. The need seems to be to listen. Start there. Say, "Lord, I am speechless at this time." As far as He is concerned, that may be the best prayer you have prayed in a long time. We often talk too much. In that prayer time, listening to God could constitute the entire prayer. Devotion to listening to God can reveal much about you. In those moments you do out of need what the Psalmist admonishes you to do: "Wait on the Lord. Be of good courage, and He will strengthen thine heart. Wait I say on the Lord." [51] Urgency is the one state of mind that can handle the inevitable distractions that come during our prayer time. No matter where you are, they come.

I like nature, and frequent our cabin in the country as often as the schedule permits. Any nature lover would love this place. But distractions have a way of finding me even here. About the time I begin to meditate while sitting on the screened-in porch, a bass jumps in the lake not more than twenty-five feet away. "What's that?" I say as I jump to see the circular waters ripple away. My meditative thoughts now resemble a fish. And I don't mean that in the traditional Christian symbolic sense.

Or an armadillo lumbers across the yard with a mockingbird swooping down and attacking the intruder. Somewhere in the sentences of my prayer the words inevitably get tangled: "Father God, clear my mind of—That peckerwood's beak is going to be blunted after awhile—Give me the words that I might—What's that?" A big crane swoops in for refreshments in the lake. I start again: "Bless our congregation as we attempt to—those are the moo-ingest cows I ever heard—"

My wife, Doris, calls, "Let's eat." And then I pray the one consistent prayer of the morning. I thank God, without a distraction, for providing food.

1. *Being still and quiet does not come easy.* On Sunday morning, when you say, "Now, let us have our 'Quiet Time' for prayer," the noise level raises ten decibels. Somebody tears a sheet out of the registration book that sounds like the ripping of a king-sized bed sheet. It is never one complete tear. "Riiiiip!"—silence—"Riiiiip!"—silence—"Riiiiip!"—silence—"Riiiiip!" The last tear comes through with a clear "ip!" While that goes on, fifty to 100 people cough. Nearly as many blow noses. Inevitably, there is someone nearby clipping his finger nails. Or is he on the other side of the church? Or is he in the balcony? Trying to find the creature is like trying to find a cricket in the dead of the night. "Am I the only one who hears that noise?" you say to yourself as you try a low-angle glance to see if anybody else is as disturbed as you. All you see is the child in the front pew making faces at you.

"Maybe they don't hear the noise," you think to yourself. "My wife never hears crickets at home."

And then you say, "Amen." Thus ends your "quiet time."

I am convinced that anything can distract you from prayer. Even your prayer can distract from praying with God. Your preoccupation with words can distract from the prayer: "O God, Thou art—(or should that "Thou" be a "Thee"—etc.)." Your preoccupation with posture can distract from prayer. The temptation is to put on a holy glow, kneel at the altar, put hands together in the form of the sculptured "Praying Hands," and look humble. That countenance makes God wonder what you are up to now.

I enjoy going to the altar with my wife on Sunday evenings. We hold hands. I like that. And I believe God does too. But even then there are distractions. One of us has to signal with a squeeze of the hand that it is time to leave the altar. Whoever squeezes first *may* be breaking up the other's prayer. But we worked around that distraction easy enough. My wife is a deliberate thinker, a deliberate person. I am a speed reader, a speed pray-er. She squeezes my hand. By the time she does, I have prayed my prayer, and got two points to a three-point sermon besides.

I am convinced that distractions can come to any place where you intend to pray. I am equally convinced that, when the urgency is strong enough, you can and will pray anywhere; and, while jets thunder overhead, trucks rumble down the highway, cows moo, and finger nails "clip"—you will not hear a distraction.

2. *Some folks use prayer to inform God what is going on.* They feel He needs their evaluation, and their directions on how to handle whatever the matter may be. I remember the time a church was having extreme differences of opinions concerning which group could use certain rooms in the church plant on certain days. Would it be the children of mothers who wanted a "Day Out" or the children enrolled in a mid-week pre-school? The children were no problem, but the parents were at war. And wouldn't you know? I was the pastor destined to arbitrate a solution. President Carter's mediating the Mideast crisis between Egypt and Israel was mere child's play in comparison to the fray I was injected into. Mothers by the dozens on both sides swarmed my office. And before you knew it, it was my fault that the problem was not solved according to the demands of both sides. At least that is what I was told by glances and words. One lady who had no children in either program knew in her mind where the problem was, and began right off to correct it. "It" was

the preacher! In my office, for forty-five minutes, she worked me over. With eyes popping and tongue lashing she tore me to shreds because *I* had, in her words, acted ugly. I said nothing, but just listened. There was no time for me to say anything. I finally got a chance toward the end of her tirade, when she said, "Bob Parrott, I pray for you."

I thought, "Now, there is a sweet spirit in there somewhere." Before she could get going again, I said, "Sue [fictitious name], prayer is serious business. I appreciate anybody praying for me. Especially do I appreciate the fact that you do. Would you please pray for me now?"

I bowed my head. I hoped she had bowed hers. An eternity went by. Then she said, "Lord, Bob's mean!" And she proceeded to tell God all the ugly things she knew about me. I heard it all over again. And the Lord did too.

Not only did she bring God up to date on all that was going on, she put me straight in the process. That leads me to ask this question: Is it prayer when you instruct God what to do? I think not. Words, yes; but prayer, no. Prayer, no; but humor, yes!

3. *Many of our "honest" prayers furnish the best humor.* I could not believe my ears one night when I attended a "prayer meeting" where everybody let it all out. One lady said to another, "I must confess that I have at times had very hostile feelings toward you."

The other lady answered, "I understand perfectly what you mean. Your crude manner of dress sometimes irritates me. But I try to understand where you are coming from."

Before the first lady could make her comeback, a man said to the second lady, "I think you ladies ought to stick with dresses, and leave the slacks for the men to wear (the second lady was wearing, you guessed it, slacks). Some of you women hate living in a man's world. Yet you dress, and walk and talk, like men."

That comment ignited the discussion. They talked at the

same time, got out their "honest" feelings. It was the most "honest" prayer meeting I ever attended, and the most hostile.

I never went back to another one of those "prayer" meetings. That one bushed me. That hyper crowd almost did me in. After that one time, when any of that group asked me why I had not been back, I said, "Well, to be honest with you, I think often of your prayer group. Please keep me in your prayers."

That seemed to satisfy. I'm not sure they really wanted me there anyway. I remember a comment someone made that night about how some people "clam up in front of the preacher." If they were "clammed up" that night when I was there, what would they be like when "the preacher" was not there?

Only God knows. And I have a feeling He wishes He didn't.

When you try to impress God with your "honesty," you can be sure that He is more entertained than impressed.

4. *When you take charge of God in your prayer to Him, a ludicrous incongruity erupts.* You can see this in the cult prayer group. In this gathering one figure emerges as the thinker for the others. When one person makes all the decisions, arbitrates disagreements, and tells what must be done to make things right, you likely have run onto a prayer cult arrangement. You can be sure you have when the cult leader talks entirely around the theme: "Let us love one another." And he seems to keep looking at your wife when he says it! Oftentimes these cult prayer leaders divorce their wives because, as they put it: "Things are different in this marriage."

And he is right. In the former marriage his wife was his same age. In this marriage his new mate is twenty years his junior. She was not yet born when he married his first wife. It is strange that the *Lord* always provides younger women.

The cult leader does what too many of us do in our own

50

way. The Lord gets blamed for much of our own wrong-doing:

"The Lord has given me a taste for fine wines. I must use this talent or it will go away."

- - - - - -

"The more I am absent from the church, the fonder my heart grows. The Lord has given me much love for the church."

- - - - - - -

"The Lord has given me so much. I would like to give much of it back to Him. But if I did, He might think I am ungrateful for it. So I'll just thank Him—and keep it."

And so on the list grows. And so on we pray. And God laughs. So should we.

C. *The demonic destroyer of the human spirit is self-deception.* That subterfuge uses prayer as a means of self-aggrandizement or self-abasement, which is self-aggrandizement in reverse (if I can convince God I am no good, He will give me the attention I deserve). You can pray for reasons that sound all right, but the reasons have nothing to do with prayer—which is to know God. For instance nothing is farther from prayer than to pray in order to be a saint, or in order to be good. That is using prayer to elevate self rather than to know God.

The truth is: we barely have enough faith to keep going when the going gets rough. We are much like a neighbor we had when I was a boy. He walked five miles to work at the County Courthouse every day. Rather, he *started* to walk the five miles every day. Usually, somebody down the road would pick him up. At that point, the worst part of the day began for him. He did not like to walk all the way to work. He did not like to ride. Riding in cars scared him stiff. But he preferred what seemed like the "ride of eternity" to the long walk. As soon as he climbed into the neighbor's car, he grabbed the door handle and held on for dear life the rest of the journey. He did not talk. He looked in all directions, and held onto the door handle—ready to jump at the moment of the inevitable collision that never came. But meanwhile, he put a kink in many a car door handle and yanked one handle right out of the car! He exercised barely enough faith to get in the car. From then on he just hoped he would make it.

When you pray, start from where you are—from weakness. Try to fool God, and you make a fool of yourself. With God's help there is a way you can handle foolishness. You laugh at it.

D. *Pray to know the Truth of God.* Make that your goal, and you can know the Truth that illumines the incongruities in your prayers. *Humor can save your prayer life.*

1. *Our prayers of confession could stand some saving.* We confess that we have not loved as we ought. We confess that we have not done those things we ought to have done, and that we have done those things we ought not have done, etc., etc. And when our son or daughter calls us, we ask them to come back later. We are so busy confessing our sins that we cannot help others!

2. *Our prayers of thanksgiving and praise need more substance.* Sometimes we sound like Jonah in the belly of the big fish:

> Then Jonah prayed to the Lord his God from the belly
> of the fish, saying,
>> "I called to the Lord, out of my distress,
>> and he answered me;
> out of the belly of Sheol I cried,
>> and thou didst hear my voice.
> For thou didst cast me into the deep,
>> into the heart of the seas,
>> and the flood was round about me;
> all thy waves and thy billows passed over me.

Then I said, "I am cast out from thy presence;
how shall I again look upon the holy temple?"
The waters closed in over me,
    the deep was round about me;
weeds were wrapped about my head
    at the roots of the mountains.
I went down to the land whose bars closed upon me forever;
yet thou didst bring up my life from the Pit,
    O Lord my God.
When my soul fainted within me,
    I remembered the Lord,
and my prayer came to thee,
    into thy holy temple.
Those who pay regard to vain idols
    forsake their true loyalty.
But I with the voice of thanksgiving will sacrifice to
thee;
what I have vowed I will pay.
    Deliverance belongs to the Lord! [52]

We act like Jonah. The Lord God, whom Jonah had pro-
fusely thanked, told Jonah a second time to preach to the
Ninevites. Jonah did, and became very angry because the
people believed his message and repented!

When you pray one way and act another, you are ludicrous.

3. *We need to look with Truth at our prayers of petition.* My
experience has been—you had better watch what you pray
for. You may get it! You piously ask for faith. What you may
not realize is that, in order to know faith, you have to be
tested. You are asking for a test!

I prayed for deliverance from tobacco many years ago.
And I quit smoking. But what a test! I was sharing with a
man how, after these thirty years without smoking cigarettes,

my mouth on occasion waters when I see someone light up a cigarette. He said with an air of extreme self-confidence, "Well, I prayed for God to deliver me from the crave to smoke. And He did. People smoke around me all the time, and my mouth never waters at all."

I marvelled at the man's obvious super self-control. And then one night at a church softball game I noticed, as he pitched the ball, his jaw was swollen. Between some of the pitches he spat an awful wad of residue on the ground. I supposed in some way that relieved the pain. Then as he walked from the mound I saw him take his medicine from Beechnut chewing tobacco. No wonder his mouth never watered at the sight of a cigarette smoker. It was too full of Beechnut juice!

a. *The agnostic might say that the prayer of petition merely expresses autosuggestion.* The prayer of petition goes farther than that. The prayer of petition relies on theosuggestion—on God. Theosuggestion, however, does include a dimension of autosuggestion. It has to because the truth is: autosuggestion works. Concentrate on lowering your blood pressure, and the pressure goes down. Concentrate on lowering your body temperature, and your body temperature goes down. Concentrate on relaxing your spastic colon, and your colon settles down. Concentrate on relaxing the brain, and the migraine headache goes away, etc., etc. Any prayer that expresses truth is to that extent theosuggestion. Theosuggestion includes autosuggestion. When you accept autosuggestion as God-given, you have graduated from autosuggestion to theosuggestion—to the knowledge that all Good comes from God, who is Good. Further, your autosuggestion now contains a belief. A faith. Now autosuggestion becomes transformed by your faith in God. The prayer of petition, then, becomes theosuggestion. That God-in-it dimension of our petitions makes what God wants what we want.

In the light of what has been said, you can see how we

often reduce our prayers of petition to mere autosuggestion. And that act of trying to pass autosuggestion off as theosuggestion seems ludicrous. A big part of the fun in watching a football game comes not during the contest, but in the quiet huddle before the opening kickoff, when the team "prays" for strength and health and will to win the game (it is especially incongruous when they "pray" for the *other* team). Then, like a huge firecracker, they explode with a wild shout that startles every angel in Heaven, and run onto the field like charged-up wild buffalo. At which time the fans yell, "Nail him!" "Run over him!" and "Hit 'em again, harder! Harder!"

A boxer kneels in his corner, prays, genuflects, jumps up, flexes his muscles, and proceeds to pound his opponent senseless. His glove cuts the opponent's eyebrow. He goes for the cut over the eye. The blood flows. Finally the bruised, bloody opponent goes to the canvas. The jubilant victor drops to his knees. Prays. Genuflects. He has "petitioned." He has "thanked." He tries to pass autosuggestion off as theosuggestion. And it is ludicrous.

b. *Too often we look upon the prayer of petition as an outgrowth of our "buddy-system" with God*—with Him as our little-bitty buddy! He is there to save us when we need Him. Otherwise He is free to do as He pleases.

For others of us God is the Power Supply that we plug into whenever we wish. This is not too often because we act pretty powerful on our own.

Or we become so expert in our own brand of religiosity that our own "Gawdliness" keeps us from knowing God. When we become, in our own minds, prayer experts, *our* prayer becomes the end of our attention, rather than God Himself. And that is the sin of prayer-olatry.

c. *The best way to get what you need is not to ask for it primarily for yourself, but to ask for it for others.* You want someone to love you. Then pray for love to come into their lives—give them peace—give them direction. That puts you in a receptive frame of mind when they turn in your direction. The self-pity that you expressed in the words, "Nobody loves me," now gives way to your total attention being upon the other who needs love. Your prayer to God will affect Him in a thousand ways. One of these ways is: in praying to know God, you find yourself going out in love to Him. You need to go out to Him as much as you need His love coming back. The two needs are really one. When we pray for another, we lay down the track for that one to come back.

We see this sublime truth working in Moses. Moses says: "Yet now, if thou will forgive their sin—; and if not, blot me, I pray thee, out of thy book." [53]

In your prayers of petition *for* God you get Whom you ask for. And can get more. You can get a laugh at your ludicrous self. That is a reward that you would do well to accept.

4. *You would think that prayers of intercession are outside humor.* After all, we are thinking of others—but are we? Since intercessory prayers are prayers of petition for others, they remain *our* petitions. And anytime the self gets involved, something self-centered is likely to creep in. When that happens, the setting is humorous. For instance, you read where Peter was imprisoned by Herod. His friends prayed for his release. An angel of the Lord rescued Peter. After his release, Peter went to the house of Mary (the mother of John Mark) where they were inside at that very moment praying for Peter's release from prison. Peter knocked on the door. Rhoda recognized Peter's voice, and in her excitement left him standing at the gate while she ran to tell the others. When she told them that Peter was at the door, they said, "You are mad. It is his angel." Peter kept knocking. They left their prayer meeting where they were praying for his release, and went to the door. They opened the door and said, "Peter, what are you doing here?" [54] Their fervent prayers remained just that—*their* prayers!

a. *In our prayers we take ourselves too seriously,* and do not take God seriously enough. That condition constantly makes our prayer life the setting more for humor than for the real thing. It bothers me when someone asks me to intercede on their behalf for something that even I (much less God!) am not sure is best for them. For instance, when the young lady came to me asking me to pray that she be accepted into a certain college, I felt her petition was legitimate. And then she continued, "There is the cutest boy going there that I have met, and I want to get to know him better." Up until that moment, I thought colleges were where you went in order to learn.

Strange things take place in some prayer meetings, like the one where the deacons of the church met to pray about whether their preacher ought to go or stay. They gathered (they said) to seek God's will in the matter. That was a legitimate purpose. On the way to the prayer meeting one deacon stopped by and told the preacher: "You'd better start packing." The preacher had heard of those kinds of "prayer meetings" before, and knew the deacon was right. Sure enough, when they met and prayed over the matter, they felt "led" to ask for the preacher's resignation. They used the "prayer meeting" as a rubber stamp of approval on what they had already decided.

The intercessory prayer gets shaky when *you* intercede into the situation of the person for whom you pray—when you feel you have control of all the factors—when you feel you know more than God knows—when you feel that maybe God has not kept up with things as well as you have, and thus needs your keen insights.

b. *Jesus Christ,* because He was God, *had the capacity to intercede on behalf of all mankind.* He could love all mankind in a deeply personal way. Because He could love each person in all mankind in a personal way, He genuinely prayed to the Father for their sakes. He empathized with the people before He effectively interceded with the Father on their behalf.

"I pray not that thou shouldest take them out of the world, but that thou shouldest keep them from evil.

—Sanctify them through thy truth: thy word is truth." [55]

While no other human besides Jesus Christ is able to feel person-to-person with a world of people (a thing called sin, a broken-off-ness from who you ought to be, robs you of this ability), with the help of the Holy Spirit, the Spirit of Jesus Christ, you are able to express kindness, regardless of who is the recipient. It is kind to pray for those whom you do not know.

It would be better still for you to know those for whom you pray. The better you know them, the more they become a part of you, of your concerns, of your aspirations, of your loyalties. The greater the part they play in your life, the greater the intensity of your intercessory prayer for them. The bottom line is: when *you* have an investment in the intercessory prayer, the level of concern is at its highest.

This means that your devotional life interlocks with the needs of those out there in the world. You can pray for the poor out of the kindness of your heart. And you can contribute some way to alleviate general hardships. But your prayer for the poor intensifies in its concern when you know the poor.

c. *The way you pray says far more about you than it does about God.* Some are so confused in their relationships with God that they intercede *for* God *to* God. You have heard it said in prayer: "We pray, O Lord, that God will hear our prayers. In this time our Father we need God to help us, etc." In these instances, people are asking God to intercede for God! Now that confuses the mind of man. No telling what it does to God! God does not need us to intercede on

58

His behalf. He can care for Himself. We are not His care-takers. We need Him to intercede for us and ours; we need His care.

True intercession for another means much to the pray-er. The more you put yourself into the world of other people, and permit them in yours, the more involved you are in your prayers of intercession for them.

In prayers of intercession you are, beyond your prayers for somebody else, asking for God. You know that He can do for others what you alone cannot do for them. This prayer of intercession becomes then a prayer of dependence on God.

In the more intense prayers of intercession for *others,* when you agonize in prayer for their good, it is not only you who pray, but God Himself who prays through you. Jesus interceded on God's behalf for Simon Peter: "I have prayed for you that you fail me not." [56] "There is none good, but the Father," [57] said Jesus. That God-Spirit moves your spirit as you (God and you) pray in One Spirit (His Spirit) the inter-cessory prayer for others. That deepest experience of prayer ceases to be spoken, but is expressed through moans of the Spirit. "Likewise the Spirit also helpeth our infirmities: for we know not what we should pray for as we ought; but the Spirit itself maketh intercession for us with groanings which cannot be uttered." [58]

E. In this concluding statement of Part II, let it be re-minded that *your devotion time is a time set aside for God.* That means that God is in charge. If you really believe that, then accept whatever happens during that time as something that God can use to get to you. When you see in this light whatever interferes with your devotions, that interference, along with everything else you do, becomes God's means of communicating His Presence to you. I remember how dra-matically this Truth came home to me through our church maid, Ura Dee Jacobs. She was a delight anytime and any-where you saw her. The halls of the church reverberated with

59

Ura Dee's laugh. The toothless, grinning, little black lady had a smile for everybody. And she laughed at incongruities that those of us who take ourselves too seriously could never see. I liked Ura Dee, but I would have never known her if she had not interfered with my Sunday morning devotional time. One Sunday morning, around 7:00 A.M., she knocked on my study door. When I said, "Come in," she came in with a cup of coffee. That "intrusion" started the most beautiful revelation in my devotional life that God ever gave me (or that I recognized). Once she was in the study, God took over through her. She would point her finger in my face and say, "You are God's man. Preach today what He tells you. And you listen!" She preached to me. She would act out her sermons. One day she said, "Watch those cat-walkin' folks. They's up to no good," as she walked across the floor, sashaying like a cat delicately placing one foot before the other in a manner that suggested smug self-importance. Since that time, I keep close watch on cat-walkin' folks.

She had an uncanny ability to know what was going on at the church. She never asked, never gossiped. But she knew. All you could accuse her of was: she laughed a lot. Sometimes I felt like her laugh was God's way of saying, "Aha, I see what you are up to." God was saying through her that He found out what was going on. When she heard a baby cry while a mother was busy doing something *important,* she laughed. The baby then smiled. And the mother noticed the change of Spirit in her child. Then the mother returned to some conversation about somebody who was not doing something right. And Ura Dee walked away laughing.

She laughed while washing windows that had smudges from dirty hands. "What kind of minds made these dirty smudges?" she must have asked. While sweeping up tobacco ashes that some forgot to leave outside before they went inside to hear about the body being the temple of the Spirit, she laughed. While mopping up spilled soft drinks that

60

dozens of feet had tracked through on their way to Sunday School, she laughed. She laughed at the Sunday School teacher who would not speak to her on the way to her classroom. She recognized hundreds of incongruities that the average churchgoer, who took himself seriously in all things, would never see. She laughed the laugh of God.

You can see that when Ura Dee came during my devotion time on Sunday morning, it was God saying "Good morning" to me, preaching to me, praying for me. The person there was not merely Ura Dee. She was God's spokesperson for my life. And during those years, she was *the* topmost authority of my life. No theologian, no preacher, no friend, nobody had such sweeping influence on my life as Ura Dee. I could never share this with her. If I had, it would have scared her, and she would have never returned. During those times, when she walked into my devotions, I never talked. I just sat behind my desk and listened. Many mornings after she left, I would say to God, "Thank you for coming to me in such a dramatic way. It was beautiful!" She always spoke the Truth in Love. Through her, I could see how perfectly Jesus was the Incarnate Son of God. She was to me. But that is the way Jesus said the Spirit would come. In those moments she was the Spirit of Truth incarnate for me.

When Ura Dee died, I preached her funeral. She called me her "pastor." Little did she know that she was my pastor. In that little country church that day for her funeral there were about eighty blacks and a dozen whites. In that moment of worship we were all one in the Spirit—God's Spirit. It was the hardest funeral I ever preached. I was burying my *pastor.* I would miss those "intrusions" on Sunday mornings, those laughs during the week. But something happened in the service that day. I started from absolute weakness. This avenue-in-person to God was gone. I ached. Then I said, "I want to share with you here today something about my relationship with Ura Dee. You think I was her pastor. Well, I

61

am here to tell you that she was mine." The people said, "That's right," "Amen," and "Hallelujah." Now I was not used to that kind of response to my preaching. For a moment I was taken back. Then I "heard" someone laugh; not in the church, but in my soul. I knew who it was. Then I got into the rhythm. I preached "the God" to the people that Ura Dee had preached to me. And that was a day of victory.

I do miss her "intrusions" on these Sunday mornings. But I have reminders of her presence—her Bible, her tithe book (she tithed to our church). In it she entered $6.91, $9.54, etc. (and some people find it difficult to figure out what a tithe is!). During every Sunday morning devotional time I think of Ura Dee Jacobs—how God visited me through her—and the awareness of God's Presence comes to me again. I blink a bit and swallow hard. In the two morning services that I preach following those experiences, I know a Power that works wonders. But when I take pride in my accomplishment of a great sermon, someone comes along and says something like, "I enjoyed your *effort.*" My feathers fall. But then I hear a laugh. I know who it is. And what it is. It is the laugh of God.

PART III

HUMOR IN
PASTORAL CARE

HUMOR IN
PASTORAL CARE

When you know yourself in the manner described in Part I and Part II of this book, the care you possess for others is a gift from God. When you see your own incongruities, your own imperfections, your own inadequacies, and are humbled before God who loves you *in spite of,* you care. You care for yourself. You care for others. Thus pastoral care for others begins with God's care for you, and you for yourself. If God can love *you,* you can love anybody. That kind of self-understanding breeds care for others. And permits a sense of humor in the process.

A. Since the basis for our understanding humor is ontological, *a metaphysical definition of pastoral care is in order.* In this sense *pastoral care* could be described as a care that exudes a deep sense of well-being. That sense of well-being comes from Being-itself, which through the pastor reveals a God-given care beyond the distorted motives that plague the human family. When you try to pass distorted motives off as if they were of God, the gap is obvious, and unintended humor is readily available.

1. *The incongruities in humanity are in us too.* How many times have you made a "pastoral" call, and as you press the doorbell button, hope they are not at home; or if they are in

the hospital, hope they are asleep or in the bathroom? It is much simpler to leave your calling card. To call this a "pastoral" call is ludicrous. But that is the message of this book. The ludicrous makes up a much larger part of life than we would like to admit. A preacher would grow in favor with his congregation if he would have humor-at-self. He may not be the best preacher in the world. But he would be an honest one!

This *pastoral care* in its metaphysical sense covers any arena where the preacher interfaces with one or more of his parishioners and expresses for them a Godly care, a sense of well-being that comes to them from God's Grace. The setting would include the pulpit-preaching situation (Part VI discusses this setting).

2. *Pastoral care* can take place in an office, on the street, in the pulpit—wherever you are. *Oftentimes* it *happens on the telephone.* Telephone counseling presents itself in a variety of conversations—if you are sensitive. And in those moments humor may or may not be applicable. If the caller is emotionally embroiled in the problem, and thinks only in terms of the seriousness of the tragedy, even though you see the incongruities, humor would be a risk. It is better for you to listen, sensing the incongruities, but not exposing them through laughter. The person-in-tragedy would never see the humor, and would possibly feel laughed *at.* If you should see the incongruity, laugh *at* him, and then try to explain why you were laughing *at* him, he will feel judged and put down, and will not likely see the humor. Later, when the person sees his own incongruity and laughs at himself, you may join *with* him in the humor, and relate how God loves us anyway. To use humor in that moment over the phone would be too much of a gamble.

The unexpressed sense of humor on your part in this serious conversation serves a purpose for you. It keeps you at a distance from the tragedy. If you get too seriously involved with your counselee, *you* may end up going to a counselor, who hopefully will have a sense of humor (of objectivity), and will not get too caught up in your despondency! If everybody loses his sense of humor, nobody can help anybody.

The first thing to remember about the caller who calls because he wants your prayers for somebody else is—*the caller needs your help!* He is so concerned that he had to call. You would be wise to speak to that concern.

You *may* speak to the caller through humor. Whether you do or do not is a judgment call under Truth. Once I received a caller who said, "Are you doing something important?"

I said, "Nothing is more important than talking to you." He laughed because he knew that hyperbole was far from the stark truth. The incongruity was obvious. And his laugh helped him live with the fact that he was not *that* important. But he loved the comment I made. And he had no intentions of closing the gap of that incongruity. He enjoyed the hyperbole, and he did not dwell on what the illumined incongruity, the humor, really said about his true condition.

It would be the voice of nothingness if you told him the straight "Truth" of how important he really was. Alas, that would destroy him. The incongruity illumined by Truth is the only expression proper for him in that moment. Straight "truth" would be a lie (a masquerade of truth) because it kills when told. A laugh with Truth is the acceptable way that we incongruent preachers can work with incongruent parishioners, and they with us.

3. *You've seen preachers who counsel people to tears* in the study, in the hospital, on the street, in the pulpit, and on the telephone. They are so dead-serious in dealing with the troubled soul's problem that they become a problem. It is at this point that one of counseling's biggest fallacies takes place. If you, the counselor, feel that with enough probing conversation you can pinpoint "the problem," you play the *hubris* game. You soar with the gods and set yourself up as the

object of unintended humor. Help comes from you, the pastor/counselor, not when you practice your psychological theory on your "patient," but when you *are* a friend who listens, cares, witnesses, and prays with your troubled parishioner. "What you *are* speaks louder than what you say" is an ontic statement that works in the counseling situation.

When you and the troubled person put your minds to the problem, and wrestle in the mud of the despairing situation, you are relying on your own abilities to observe, diagnose, and remedy. No human has that kind of supernatural power. To act like you do, and take yourself seriously in the process, serves to widen the gap of your incongruity, the gap that is illumined by Truth.

4. In counseling, *you can better solve the problem* not by putting your full attention on the problem, but by *appealing to Truth,* the Spirit that gives meaning and validity to all of life's situations. Without Truth you tend to justify actions according to your own whims and prejudices. That leads to the final triumph of tragedy. There is no humor *in* tragedy. I remember the time a minister, who had his master's degree in counseling from a leading accredited seminary, came to talk to me about his problem. He had attempted suicide, and from his hospital bed came to know me through our church's televised Sunday worship service. As I talked with this professional counselor, a reason for the high suicide rate among psychiatrists surfaced. The man had so completely identified with his counselee, one who had attempted suicide because of a love affair gone bad, that he "fell in love" with her. He left his wife in order to marry this woman. Now she would not marry him. And he could not handle the rejection. As I recall our conversation, the man's mind/emotions were so entrenched in this complex problem that he could not (or would not) see where he was under Truth. He justified every decision/act that put him where he was. I could see his incongruities, but any laugh from me would have been a laugh

at him. It would serve only to hurt. I could not laugh with him at himself because he had shut out Truth. After two more attempts at taking his life, he succeeded. Stark tragedy prevailed.

When his mother came later to talk with me, she related how her son had such a wonderful sense of humor (she did not know about his tragic involvement with a counselee). She could not comprehend how he, of all people, could take his own life. She was right in her thinking. If he could have looked at his tragic involvement at a distance, and sensed with Truth his incongruities, and laughed at *himself,* he might be alive today.

His mother recalled happier days. She laughed quietly— between sobs. But she laughed. This was a signal from God that He was redeeming her.

> Since the non-being of pride (who we think we are) plays a part in humor, there always remains that tragic aspect of humor. Pride boasts our self-importance while truth reveals what we are really like. The incongruity may ripple into wit, wrinkle into irony, or erupt in laughter (or tears). Whichever the case, pride is revealed for what it really is, and the *imago dei* is revealed for what human nature essentially is: making humor potentially redemptive in pointing one to one's true self. Insofar as humor does help one rise above the tragic, humor participates in this genuine paradox in the form of redemption.[59]

As you look at the minister/counselor's tragic predicament, you can see the incongruity—he counseled her into her bedroom! A warning flag for all counselors goes up at this point! Stay behind the desk! I remember a college professor who was forced to resign his position on a university faculty and leave the state because he left his chair behind his desk,

69

and went around to where the young co-ed was seated. In her words, he "placed his hands where they had no business being." In his words (I can still see him pacing nervously back and forth in my office), he said, "I just barely placed my hand on her shoulder." It is hard to reach her shoulder from behind the desk. Stay behind the desk!

B. Normally you think of pastoral care in terms of the serious—of caring for the sick, counseling the troubled, marrying the young, burying the dead, etc. Those functions of the minister deal directly with the tragic in human life. *Incongruities exist within the fabric of these tragic settings.* Make a place for humor in all areas of pastoral care. The minister must realize that, during these somber, sometimes morbid, situations, a pleasant manner manifests good humor and can in itself bring healing to the broken-spirited.

The first thing you can do to develop that sense of incongruities is take a look at yourself in your role as pastor. Do you take yourself too seriously in that role? If you do, you are taking the wrong situations seriously. That incongruity is itself good for a laugh on any given day. I know a preacher who left the pastoral ministry in order, in his words, "to devote my full time to the ministry of counseling." When he made that transition, *he* changed. His voice dropped to low, lugubrious tones that told you how seriously he took himself. And he obviously hoped you would take him as seriously as he took himself. Maybe he does help his clients. People who enter his office will soon see that this man's sense of gloom is far worse than theirs. And *that* has to be reassuring!

The same Truth that reveals God's love and concern also reveals our incongruities when we act like what we are not—when we *act* like we are concerned. That same Truth is healing for the troubled soul. It is the "bottom line" that you search for in counseling. It is the light that shines on the gap of incongruities, that provides for the periodic laughs while you are on the way to helping the counselee see the "bottom line." Truth reveals the *straight* and the *comic* in the same dynamic process of counseling. Humor then becomes an integral part of truth therapy.

C. *Truth therapy is the most powerful therapy of all.* What is the most powerful input in a counseling situation? The genius of the counselor? No. He may have suicidal tendencies. The counselee? No. He is there because he is shaky. The most powerful input into a counseling situation is Truth, the Holy Spirit.

> There can be no humor without truth. Whether in finitude or sin-in-finitude, it is truth which is breaking into situations on earth through humor, occasioned by incongruities in human life. We have seen the non-being of pride. Truth, as a divine dispensation revealing the being of God, which we call Being-itself, shows up pride for what it *is—not.* God conquers pride when we know the truth.[60]

1. All *pastoral care should be designed as a response to God's Truth.* That spiritual posture of the pastor works anywhere for the parishioner. And for the pastor! It frees you from *having* to succeed in your pastoral ministry. You do not have to make the success-or-failure judgment on yourself concerning any pastoral event. Your image of your own success or failure can hardly be described as objectve—as an absolute expression of truth. You may not use in a pastoral event the best technique, but when you do your best in helping someone know the truth, you *are* a success.

2. *A pastor does not have to succeed if he is a success.* A successful pastor depends on Truth to carry him into a crisis situation, and to bring him out. Truth has the power to do that. And it often uses humor in the process. While writing

this chapter, I consciously looked for moments that illustrated the role humor plays in the ongoing process of counseling. On one occasion, the "bottom line" came to the troubled counselee. He recognized that his problem was his thinking. He thought everything through so carefully that he drove his wife up the wall and then out of the house. He meticulously picked out her faults for me (after he had picked them out for her!). And he even proceeded to pick out his own. He evaluated everything very objectively, very thoroughly. And he assumed that since *he* was a careful thinker, *he* was right. He came to realize that his thinking, rather than trusting and loving, was his problem. He actually verbalized that "bottom line" with the comment: "It looks like I need to love more and think less." Following that comment, our conversation trailed off in another direction. And then, upon his leaving, I said: "It just does not pay to think that we can provide our own destiny."

He said: "Well, I'll have to think about that!"

3. *Problem-oriented therapy depresses.* If you put your whole attention upon forgetting a worry, you remember it every time you try to remember to forget it! But when you put your mind on the Truth, you see with Truth incongruities that elicit a laugh—a laugh that frees and redeems.

A baby is born a reactionary (reacts to needs, e.g. sleep, food). Soon the child develops the ability to make choices. Then the person learns that choosing one's own destiny (with no outside interference) may lead to fame, riches, power, and death. The psychological/spiritual plunge comes in the twinkling of an eye. A consciousness of nothing (non-being) translates itself in words such as, "I feel like hell," or "I've nothing to live for," or "Nothing makes sense." These wrong choices make us prisoners of the self. The self is finite and temporary.

Death inevitably results. On the other hand, choosing God's will brings freedom. We cannot know freedom until we know the Truth of God: "Know the truth and the truth will make you free." [61]

And when we know the Truth, we know the power that spotlights the gaps and elicits the humor. Only in a state of freedom, then, can we see the humor. A free spirit senses incongruities. When we are imprisoned within our own selves, we see life "straight." When we are free under God's Truth, we can see incongruities, ours as well as others. This new-found freedom does not give serenity and protection from every disturbance. Quite the contrary, awareness of a new magnitude undreamed comes with this freedom.[62]

A woman once talked with me about her divorce trauma. She had read in my book, *Ontology of Humor,* that distance from the tragic event permits one to see the incongruities. By self-transcendence we can be removed far enough from these areas to laugh.

She said, "Do you think I will ever look back on this and laugh?"

I said, "You chuckled when you asked the question. You are laughing now."

She unconsciously saw the incongruity. The fact that she could ask the question with a chuckle indicated a "removal" from the intensity of her trauma. This "distance" permitted her to laugh while embroiled in the tragedy. She had, just prior to this question, told how her husband loved his golf. She said, "He kisses the golf ball more than he kisses me!"

4. In a counseling situation, *the recognition of an incongruity can lead to a straight recognition of the Truth* in the situation. This manner of interpretation is superior to a purely rational approach. Reasoning alone leads the conver-

sation down a plane based on misconception. What you say is "out there" is not "out there" at all.

> The way in which we happen to see and feel things is the result of the peculiarities of our nervous systems. These are "sights" we cannot see and, as even children know today with their high-frequency dog whistles, "sounds" we cannot hear. It is absurd, therefore, to imagine that we ever perceive anything "as it really is." [63]

This being the case, a counselor and a counselee may spend a whole session seriously probing into "what's wrong," and justify whatever conclusions that coincide with the premises with which they began. This method was used by a clergyman/counselor as he counseled some women with marital problems. He first established that their sex life was inadequate. From that point on he encouraged them to have sex with him in order to locate their weaknesses, and make changes that would please their husbands and in turn help their marriages. When some of them tried this therapy, and then told their husbands, the husbands were not able to understand the rationale. But the counselor understood the thinking of the husbands when they descended on him. He decided to take his practice to another city.

5. *Empathy to the point of emotional involvement can send the pastor/counselor into the pits.* I have to watch myself during times of people's grief. My sympathy carries me too far. For instance, there was the time the old fella lost his wife of over forty-five years. His intense grief shattered me. Uncontrollably, he told over and over how much she meant to him. On the day of the funeral, I tried to comfort him with words. But no words seemed to work. He mourned and mourned

and mourned. I did too. His grief was the saddest occasion of my life.

Three weeks later he walked up to the door of the parsonage and rang the doorbell. I opened the door. He said, "Preacher, meet my bride-to-be!"

Sure enough, a few days later I read the vows for the man and his bride. *He* was happy, and I still had not shaken my grief over *his* loss of his first wife. I performed the ceremony. But to be honest with you, I felt like shooting him!

6. In many instances *you can tell whether the counselee is honest* in his search for the Truth *by monitoring his willingness to laugh* at his incongruities. If he insists on justifying his incongruent actions, you can be sure he will not see nor admit the Truth of his situation. Sometimes parishioners seek counsel from the pastor in order to make themselves feel that they have made a stab at solving the problem. They do this without any intention of changing. Rather than laugh at their incongruities, they seriously justify their actions. Take for instance the wife who filed for divorce and then sought "counseling" that agreed with her decision to marry another man. She said she and her new love had prayed, and that God had blessed their decision to divorce their spouses and marry each other. When asked if God had blessed this, she said, "Yes." She was dead-serious. When you take, as this woman did, incongruities as if they were the straight Truth, there is no redemption. But there is humor midst the tragedy.

7. Since everybody is not as he ought to be and does not act as he ought to act in every situation, you try to help the troubled soul see that *an act of perfection is not the same as perfection.* An act of self-despising gets one nowhere. No one can be *that bad!* Some acts of self-denial may be as funny as one thinks they are serious. "To deny oneself, in the Christian sense, is not to despise or contemn the self; actually, of course, self-disparagement is an inverted form of pride. (The

75

easy test of this is to agree with another's self-disparaging verdict on himself as if it were sincere and realistic.)" [64] If the troubled soul could see the incongruities of specific actions of the people involved in the tragic situation, the glimpse of the gaps between *what is* and how one acts like *what is* (the humor) can lead the person to the straight comment concerning their problem. That universal "bottom line" comment is: "That is true."

The laugh can help the person see the Truth and acknowledge it. Through the same Truth that illumined the incongruities, one may be led to accept the transforming grace of God that heals. And that is no laughing matter.

Every troubled person is anxious about something. He expresses this anxiety in some concrete form—He did not get his promotion—His wife has left him—His children have moved away, etc. "Generally the threat of meaninglessness is experienced negatively as a threat to the existence of the self—. But when this form of anxiety is confronted affirmatively—when the individual both realizes the threat of meaninglessness and takes a stand against the threat—the result is a strengthening of the individual's feeling of being a self, a strengthening of his perception of himself as distinct from the world of non-being, of objects." [65] One of the strongest stands against the threat of meaninglessness expressed in anxiety is a sense of humor. When you laugh at incongruities that are in conjunction with the threat, the anxiety decreases in its intensity. I saw this happen in an employee who knew that an impending firing of employees would include him. At one point his anxiety caused him to question his sense of self-worth. That question shrank in importance as he handled his problem with a sense of humor. Statements like "Once you let me go, there's no second chance for you to get me back. Don't even ask me!" (as if the employer were going to!) relieved him of much anxiety in that unstable job situation. The fact that he did not let his boss hear that bit of humor saved his job far beyond his expectations!

"God accepts us as we actually are—not the ideal self we wish we were nor the denigrated self we despise ourselves for being. It is this actual, imperfect self which we have come to know in genuine contrition, that God takes as the *object* of His transforming grace. Wherefore, we may accept ourselves as the *subjects* of grace." [66]

8. *Truth therapy reveals care.* This *involves listening, sharing, reminiscing, witnessing, and being in a common search for Truth.*

This comes off positive where the "I feel that you feel" non-directive technique often comes off negative. You can feel the negative coming on in a conversation that goes something like this:

Counselee: "I feel awful bad about my short temper."

Counselor: "I feel that you feel awful bad about your short temper."

Counselee: "Yes, that is what I said."

Counselor: "I feel that you feel that is what you said."

Counselee: "I am not sure that you feel what I am saying."

Counselor: "I feel that you feel that I don't feel what you are saying."

And the troubled soul leaves feeling numb with the lack of understanding on the part of such a "feeling" pastor.

Far more realistic to life than any techniques of counseling is a pastor's heart open to Truth in a conversation that includes listening and talking, reasoning and relaxing, and laughing through tears. A laugh *with* a troubled soul at incongruities can be spotted by one caught in the most tragic circumstance. A recognized incongruity may lead one to accept the Truth that illumined the incongruity in the first place. And that illumines the "bottom line" of the problem faced. You can see the pattern developing in your counseling situation in the manner it happened in this one. The man was now in his second marriage. I had counseled him and his bride, and had performed the ceremony. He now sat in my office telling me how difficult this wife was to live with. He wanted me to help him patch up their problems. He really seemed to want this marriage to work. He explained in detail her bad habits. After each of her bad habits had been thoroughly explored, he looked down in a casual manner, paused a bit, and began again on another weakness that possessed his wife. After a while, during one of his downcast pauses, I asked him, "What are you looking at?"

He answered, "I've got a list of those things that my wife does that are crazy."

I said, "You mean you are reading from a list of her faults. And you want your marriage to work?"

He said, "You don't understand. I have such a poor memory that if I didn't write them down, I would forget them!" He could not remember the worries that he wanted to forget if he did not write them down!

—In a few moments, the Truth illumined for him his incongruity. A slight grin came across his face. The tragic seriousness of his shattered marriage now was seen in a sense of humor toward himself. That was the last time I saw him in a counseling situation. And his marriage has lasted eighteen years at the time of this writing.

Another time I recall a couple with teenage children had divorced. A trail of tragic circumstances had led them to my office. He had an affair with another woman. When his wife found out, she shot him with a shotgun. After his hospital stay, they went to court. All the sordid details made the front page of the local newspaper. They had talked only over the telephone. Now they faced each other to probe their problems. The fact that they were in my office revealed that Truth was already working in their hearts and minds. But those first few minutes were serious to the point that a quarrel was brewing.

"Do you really want to be reconciled?" I asked.

She said, "I love him, but . . ."

With the pain of a yet-to-be-healed wound showing in his face, he said to her, "You sure have a strange way of showing it! If you love me now and would shoot me, what would you do if you didn't love me?"

She grinned and said, "I'm sorry."

Rational explanation cannot explain the laughter that possessed all three of us at the incongruities of two people who had said in days past that they loved each other, but in deed denied it. It was difficult for him to explain to his wife how much he loved her while he was having an affair with another woman. It was difficult for her to explain how she shot him because she loved him. From their Truth-illumined incongruities, they turned to Truth Himself, namely God. And at a later date, in sublime worship, they were once again married. I performed the ceremony. For many years now they have been in their words, "happier than ever before." Both carry the scars of a tragic history, but they laugh through their tears.

You can tell in counseling situations when, after a laugh at incongruities, the troubled souls have recognized the "bottom line" of their problem. Inevitably then they will say, "That is true."

9. *Truth is already working in the troubled parishioner's mind.* A pastor/counselor simply permits it to come out. The mental posture is listening to Truth, not evaluating the facts.

Pastor Charles L. Allen practices Truth therapy by asking a troubled person questions. The first is: "What is your problem?" The troubled soul goes to great length getting out the problem. Then Dr. Allen asks, "What are you going to do about it?" The person tells him, and before leaving, thanks him for his advice!

In your conversation with your troubled parishioner, be alert to his/her un-self-conscious comment: "That's true." That outcropping comment reveals that the greatest positive power in a counseling situation is over-riding the greatest negative power, the power of non-being, nothingness.

If the last words of a counseling situation by the counselee are "That's true," then you know that a solution has been offered by God.

10. God's Truth is stronger in the lives of the suffering than you ever dreamed, or will ever know. Truth is infinite. Our minds cannot reach that far. We cannot know that, but we can faith it. *Faith puts you into the mode of being a pastor wherever you are.* The hospital is one place where that *modus operandi* works. You do not have to be a pastor for that faith to work; but if you are a pastor, you *are* because that faith in Truth gives you the sense of *being* a pastor.

It was not my keen awareness of the events in the life of that woman on the elevator in a Houston, Texas, hospital that evoked the healing for that hour. It was Truth. You can see it working. As we stood on one of the higher floors waiting for the elevator, I saw her standing alone and said, "What would we do without Christ?" She began talking about her sick husband and her sense of being lost in the big city. The elevator opened. We got on. She still talked about her sick husband, the big city, her hopes, and her prayers. She talked all the way down to the main lobby. As we exited, she was still talking. Before we parted, she shook my hand and said, "Thanks for talking with me!"

And all I did was listen. But to her my listening was talking. And essentially it was. It was conversation. She felt a care that *spoke.*

11. In the instance previously mentioned, my "counseling"

came from simply *being* there and caring. At first glance this sounds more like an accident than skill. Not so. *It takes skill to know when to be quiet.*

Wayne Oates is right when he says:

> The pastor, regardless of his training, does not enjoy the privilege of electing whether or not he will counsel his people. . . . His choice is not between counseling or not counseling, but between counseling in a disciplined and skilled way and counseling in an undisciplined and unskillful way.[67]

The pastor as counselor becomes ludicrous when he lets his discipline and skill show, e.g., when he points to his degree on the wall and explains to the troubled soul how hard this goal of becoming a great and learned counselor was to achieve; how he has helped people for nothing in return (sounds like a boast in martyrdom); how he has conquered the Rogerian technique (he talks much about listening).

You must be skilled without letting it show. One skill that can be used is a sense of incongruities, a sense of humor. If you show what you are doing in your use of humor, you will sound more foolish than intelligent to the troubled soul. Any explanation of humor destroys it. Any effort to show your great sense of humor will destroy your credibility in the eyes of the one being counseled.

Humor is a spontaneous happening in the person glimpsing the gaps of incongruities. Reasoning begins as you suggest a turning to God who is the Truth.

In a pastoral situation, humor is not something you as a counselor have to work at or develop a technique for. Remember, do not let your skills show! It requires from you a listening ear and an awareness that God is at work illuminating incongruities. On the day of this particular writing I was called to the hospital ICU waiting room at 7:00 A.M. A member of my congregation had lost her son-in-law in an auto accident the evening before. Her daughter was near death, and her granddaughter was critically injured. In a private setting, I listened to this grandmother talk to me and another daughter—and listened to God through Truth illuminate incongruities in her mind, and release her to some extent from the dread tragedy of the moment. This is called "nervous laughter," but it is laughter nonetheless, and it is spiritual medicine in a crisis. She talked ceaselessly and laced her conversation with bits of humor through her tears. She asked me if my plane were fixed (it had been in a hangar fire). I answered, "Yes."

She then launched into a ten-minute conversation about her son, who had learned to fly at fourteen years of age, and how he joined the Army Air Force to learn to fly, how he was put to work as a mechanic at air bases over the country, how he got his discharge, moved to East Texas, and how he and his family had moved to a university town without a job, housing, and the full tuition, and how he finally got his degree. His part-time job had got him through college. With his degree in hand he was ready to get a full-time job. His boss sent word he wanted to see her son. She said, "My son gulped, and told his wife that he guessed he had done something wrong. He found his way on weak knees to the boss' office, and was ready for his medicine when the boss told him that he was to become a manager in the company. A better job than he ever hoped to find."

Admittedly this is no knee-slapping bit of humor. But the point is that this mother and daughter laughed at these events. And I laughed with them both—just before we had prayer.

This good humor from God relieved her of some of the tension. All I did was listen and watch God perform, and thank Him for His Presence in this hour of crisis.

12. *Pastoral care through humor comes directly from God.* A

sense of well-being was restored to a planeload of passengers on an airliner through a spontaneous awareness of an incongruity following a near tragic experience. The report comes from a well-known pastor aboard the plane, Bishop Finis A. Crutchfield. At its assigned altitude, the airliner cruised smoothly. The stewardesses were routinely caring for individual needs of the passengers. One man entered the restroom in the tail of the plane. Some were listening to stereo via headphones, visiting across the aisle, or reading. And then the plane hit clear-air turbulence. It nosedived out of control thousands of feet in seconds. Trays sailed. Onboard luggage flew about. Food and drinks spilled. People standing or sitting without belts buckled sailed in zero-degree gravity. People screamed. Then, as quickly as the unscheduled dive had come, smooth air returned. People sat in dumbstruck silence. And then the door to the rest room in the tail section opened. And a disheveled human being, ashen-white from the preceding event, entered the aisle to once again find his seat. The passengers had forgotten about the man. They watched the pitiful fellow make his unstable way to his seat. And then they erupted in laughter when he said loud enough for all to hear, "They ought to put seat belts on those seats!"

God, as Cosmic Ironist, provides the humor. We see this in a story told by Howard Clinebell about a little white-haired woman who had been in a mental hospital for over twenty years: "We both knew she was dying. Before I delivered a little homily to 'comfort' her, something told me to ask her how she felt about the experience she faced. Her wonderfully honest reply made my prefabricated sermonette absurdly irrelevant. She responded with intense feeling: 'Chaplain, I'll be so glad to get out of this damned place!' " [68]

Clinebell did not write that they laughed. Surely they did. And that laugh would be a release from the tension of the death situation.

We did laugh that day as the woman said about her stay in the hospital: "One good thing about it—I was so sick that they could not hurt me."

13. *There can be unintended humor in the most serious situations.* One came in a church that advertises on billboards and newspapers this motto: "Catch the glow." At the prescribed hour for a funeral service, the funeral director and the family arrived at the church, and there was no preacher. The director had the family stand at the front door of the church (the temperature was a sweltering 92°) while they looked for the preacher. It was already past the hour for the funeral service. Then the director said to one of the pall bearers who was at that moment a panicked member of the church, "Isn't that *him* sitting down there on the front row?"

The funeral director glided quickly down the side aisle, and sure enough the preacher was sitting with that far away look on his face. He forgot that he was supposed to be at the pulpit motioning for the congregation to stand at that very moment. Quickly he jumped to the pulpit and lifted his hands. The congregation stood. In came the family. All were seated. Then the preacher spoke into a mike that was not turned on. He went into a side room and switched on the P.A. system. Back to the pulpit he came, and he delivered his message. As the people left the auditorium, their eyes caught a banner draped across the balcony the width of the church with these words on it: "Go for it!"

The congregation at that funeral service did not know what they were going "for," but they had caught the glow from the preacher that day. It surely was red.

When humorous events such as these happen, you have these options: (1) Ignore them and add to the incongruity. Imagine a face that has caught the glow, the gentle, humble, sublime look of what one thinks a Christian ought to look like. If that Heavenly-minded person ignored his more sleepy-eyed, dull-witted mistakes, he would cause a monstrous incongruity. (2) Make excuses for the blunders, and add to the incongruity. Imagine that same glowing face of *Gawdly* perfection trying to explain how the janitor forgot to turn on the P.A. system, or trying to explain how at a funeral you "go for it." The more you try to justify your blunder, the greater the embarrassment of others for you! (3) Accept the Truth that illumined your incongruity and you will turn off *your* glow as you are turned *on* by the Truth: "I am not who I thought I was, but God loves me." When that awareness comes across to those under your pastoral care, they will see and know through you the Truth. They will know that, if you are loved in spite of your incongruities, they can be loved in spite of their incongruities. And that is no laughing matter. That is healing.

D. *The pastor expresses care,* not in a condescending manner ("Yes, yours is a typical low middle-class problem"), nor a fawning/pitying manner ("Oh you poor darling!"), nor a scholarly objective manner ("I'll find your problem in a minute!"), nor in a braggadocious manner ("Here's how I did it!"), but *"by being in the presence of another."* [69] A refined look at that *being* reveals incongruities. An effective pastor admits his incongruities, laughs at himself, and thereby frees the troubled soul from feeling inadequate in the pastor's presence. Care expressed in this manner comes off genuine. You are not trying to prove anything. Your incongruent self talks to an incongruent self. And you are helped in coming to be who you ought to be in the interchange just as significantly as the troubled parishioner. If you fall into the trap of using this relationship to prove you have a fine sense of humor, you have turned your *being* into acting and invite unintended humor at yourself. You are now laughable, not because of a true look at your incongruities, but because now pride uses your sense of humor. The incongruity now is: you are not as you think you are. People now laugh at you, but not for the reasons you have established in your mind. In your mind you are a master of wit; in their minds you are a master of self-delusion.

If you present yourself as a whole, congruent self to the parishioner, you come off as a superman. A god. That is an incongruity that the parishioner may never see. He may never recognize this unintended humor on your part because he is too concerned with his own problems. And your super-hold on yourself serves to intensify his own sense of inadequacies.

1. The parishioner can know you love him and accept his incongruities because *you are loved* by God and accepted by Him *in spite of your incongruities.* When you witness to the troubled soul this sense of being loved by God *in spite of,* your expression with conviction motivates that one *to be* an ongoing self in spite of the fact he is not as he ought to be, in spite of the fact he has fouled up and could do it again. You can look in your own life and identify yourself with this universal human trait. Here is how it happened to me recently. I whizzed out of my office, hurried to my car on the back parking lot, started the engine, put it in reverse, turned my steering wheel in a tight counterclockwise direction, and with my right front bumper creased the left front door of the car to my right. I tried to think of some good excuse for pulling such a boner, but I couldn't. I went back inside the church to see if someone could tell me who owned the car. No one could. So my secretary put a note under the car's windshield wiper giving my name as the door bender. We deduced that the car was driven by one of the youths who had gone with others on an all-day trip to another city. And so it was. That night when the youth group returned, the young man saw the broad well-defined dent in his door. And he immediately blamed the church custodian for damaging his car. A bit of argument ensued as the custodian explained he had been in that parking spot for a short while. "And anyway," he explained, "you can plainly see my car bumper

does not have a scratch on it. And it's a small car, and can't reach that high on your door."

The young man then went into an uncontrollable tirade: "What sorry low-down turkey did this to me and ran off?"

At that moment the custodian pointed to the note under the windshield wiper. The youth took it off and read the note: "Dr. Parrott wants the owner of this car to know that he dented your car, and wants you to know that proper repairs will be made. He apologizes for this mishap."

The young man fell silent and then said, "I think I made a mistake."

But he did not make a mistake. His pastor, on more occasions than he would like to admit, is a true-blue turkey!

2. *Pastoral care is caring for others when it seems they don't care for you.* That takes much grace. I remember the time when I was battling the fever of a kidney infection. For four days and nights it was nip and tuck trying to keep the fever down. On the fourth night at 10:00 a parishioner called and said, "Brother Bob, Grandma Jones (fictitious name) is 88 years old and is in the hospital near death. Her pastor Bro. _____ is in Hawaii and she is a devoted Primitive Baptist. But I thought I'd better call and let you know about her condition, because it may come *down to* asking you to do the funeral!"

As *down* as I felt that night, that sincere comment didn't help me. But it called the best out of me that I could muster. My answer was, "If it comes *down to* me, I'll be there!"

PART IV

HUMOR IN THE
ORDER OF WORSHIP

HUMOR IN THE
ORDER OF WORSHIP

A. At the outset of this Part IV, I want to define *two terms* that *may be used interchangeably.* Under other circumstances they could not be used interchangeably. The words are *liturgy* and *ritual. Ritual* may be the procedure used in any program, i.e., the ritual you go through when you start an airplane, and check out the controls, instruments, gas, gear, mixture, flaps, trim, prop, and run up the engine. But that ritual is not a liturgy. A ritual is made up of a procedure of events that work with any kind of program; a liturgy is made up of events in a program that relate to God in our worship of Him. Thus a liturgy is a ritual, but a ritual is not necessarily a liturgy.

You may ask, "Why use the word *ritual* at all if *liturgy* adequately takes care of the situation for the purpose of this book?" Answer: Many people use the word *ritual* when referring to *liturgy.* With this explanation the use of *ritual* as well as *liturgy* should communicate to the reader.

If you do not accept these words, then you pick whatever term you prefer to describe the events that take place when you gather for worship. All Christians do something together when they worship. You may call it "Singin' n' Prayin'," or

"Spontaneous Worship," or "the Preachin' Service." But somewhere somebody announces something, and that indicates some kind of order, whether written or oral.

1. *Orders of worship have been used since the inception of the Christian Church.* The primitive Jerusalem church had no official order. But they had an unannounced order, much of which came directly from Judaism. It was a natural thing to do since they were a Jewish sect.

> From Judaism we Christians learned the basic principles of worship, which are: adoration of the Oneness, the majesty, the glory, the holiness of God; penitence and supplication for the forgiving mercy of God; intercession for the fulfillment of God's purposes among men; thanksgiving for the good gifts and tender mercies of God to His creatures; revelation of God's character and instruction in the demands of his moral will; dedication and consecration to righteousness of life in the abiding presence and sustaining power of God's Holy Spirit.[70]

2. This Part IV is not an argument for or against liturgies, rituals, forms, or creeds. It simply asks the reader to recognize this truth: in man's serious efforts to make things right for the God/man encounter during a worship service, *God remains congruent, and man incongruent.* Nothing is laughable about God's love, truth, mercy, faithfulness, and goodness. But man, with his best intentions, is never totally what he ought to be—even in worship—and is therefore laughable when he acts like what he is not—when his "slip" shows during his effort to look his best.

Rituals as exercises in worship include everything from the silence of the Quakers (that is their ritual) to the all-inclusive prayers of Mass in the Roman Catholic Church.

The criterion that makes one liturgy superior to another

comes in the experience of the worshiper. If that liturgy (whatever it is or is not) brings an awareness of God's Presence in worship, it is the best for that person. This does not mean, however, that one will not change to a different ritual. You can be sure one will not change if a liturgy is forced on him. I have observed that one of the best ways to change others' worship habits to a more meaningful experience comes in you, the worship leader, as you reveal by action those deeper meanings that your worship ritual brings to you.

If you try to put it over in argument, you become ludicrous.

B. The order of worship is *a means by which a congregation worships God.*

> At its heart the act is *paying attention to God*—a God whom one does not see or hear or think but toward whom one may nonetheless direct his mind—and the accompaniments of worship are the reflectors which carry the mind in reciprocation back to the central object.[71]

1. As long as man has his hand in the affair, his incongruities are bound to surface. *The ludicrous appears when autonomous power creeps into the worship service,* and tries to pass itself off as theonomous power, when *you* exhibit God; i.e., when you pass your opinion off as if it were God's will—when you act humble out of pride—when you perform for the people rather than praise God—when you act like what you are not.

> Faith in anything less than Truth creates an idolatrous faith, creates an incongruity by accepting *what is not* as if it were, and sets the stage for humor that destroys the idolatrous faith. Faith in truth saves, and humor is a part of that saving process.[72]

Anyone who says, "My order of worship is the way it ought to be done in every situation," falls into this ludicrous category. That absolute attitude smacks of one whose *hubris* has gone wild.

> *Hubris* is the self-elevation of man into the sphere of the divine . . . people have identified their limited goodness with absolute goodness . . . man identifies his cultural creativity with divine creativity. He attributes infinite significance to his finite cultural creations, making idols of them, elevating them into matters of ultimate concern.[73]

And besides looking funny in his absoluteness, look at the ludicrous application of his statement. Imagine a "high church" liturgy in a remote rural setting where the people are accustomed to clapping their hands. Some unlearned graduates of seminaries have seriously tried this. The more seriously they took themselves in their efforts, the funnier it got—not in the moment, but later, when they were a bit more removed from the affair.

> Many of the subjects of adult humor are distinctly unfunny. As unpleasant as these subjects can be, there is in every one of them an element which, if we were playful, could become funny. Yet, the closer we get to the subject of the humor, the less we feel like being playful.[74]

"Thus saith the *Lord*"—that statement recognizes where power comes from.

"Thus saith *we*"—that statement assumes power to be where it is not.

Our power destroys; God's power builds.

"Thus *I* say" is an acceptable power statement once you

say it because it is expressed Truth. It is True, and not because you say it. But you say it because it is True. The courts appeal to the power of Truth in a witness, not to the power of a witness to handle Truth. They ask, "Do you swear to tell the Truth, the whole Truth, and nothing but the Truth, so help you God?" There is no whole Truth. Either it is or it isn't. And Truth, if it is the Truth, can only be "nothing but the Truth." "So help you God"—There can be no Truth without the "help" of God. God expresses who He is through Truth. Your struggle for Truth is the right struggle for Power. The Source is God.

"Thus saith the Lord" are powerful words of Grace spoken to us in the worship situation. Whether audibly or silently, the words are spoken. His Grace anticipates and initiates your prayer of confession. Stirs you to know you are loved. Haunts you until you "turn from your wicked ways." His Power makes the prayer of confession possible. Without that Power repentance turns into something you think you can do to show God how honest you are. That twist puts you in the throes of autonomous power. When you see that gap in your prayer life—when you act like you are praying as you ought, but you are not—you see unintended humor. The Truth that illumines that incongruity for you is the same Power Source that makes your prayer of confession possible.

"Thus saith the Lord" are powerful words of Grace spoken to the worshipper. This "speaking" of God's Presence evokes prayers of praise. I purposely leave out the word *adoration* because of our tendency to objectify God when we use it. It seems too easy for some to say in the same breath: "I just adore the autumn leaves, the smell of rain in a cool front, and God!" Too often we mistake an adoring look on our worshipping faces for adoration of God when in reality it is something we wear to show others how we feel about ourselves. This expression comes from the self, shows autonomous power, and provides unintended humor. Some folks practice looking holy far more than living holy. When you see that gap—when someone acts like what he is not—Truth elicits the humor.

If this tendency to misuse the word "adoration" is not yours, then use it. It is a good word if its expression for you provides for the mystery of God's Being, Being-itself.

In your prayers of petition, a feeling that you *deserve* to be heard smacks of autonomous power. And it provides the setting for humor. When you show that you know more than God about anything, you reveal the gap—you act like what you are not—and the result is humor.

Theonomous Power works wonders through prayers of intercession. In the first place it saves us from ourselves in our prayers for others. Often what we call prayers of intercession are in fact prayers of petition for self. We would not pray for others if they did not mean a lot to us. These prayers of "intercession" may be fairly selfish. When we try to pass these self-centered prayers off as if they showed absolute concern for others, oftentimes we try to prove this with an expression of self-sacrifice: "Please help them, Lord. You know I've done all I can do. My heart is broken. They won't listen to *me*. I've had all *I* can take." The moment you shove self into the picture, you once again have expressed autonomous power.

2. But when you see your incongruity, when you admit that the gap is there—that you are not who you act like, *redemption follows in the repentant spirit* of one who is now a true worshiper. Now your actions are grounded in God's Power, God's Grace. And now the order of worship has "changed" because you are changed. The responses may be the same; the hymns may be the same; the corporate prayers may be the same; but they now are channels of God's Grace, rather than the mere expressions of pride they once were.

3. Your sense of incongruities in the liturgical experience reflects a keen awareness of God's Presence. Only with His

96

Truth can you see the incongruities. Rather than an antithesis to worship, this humorous look complements the experience. God is known in a grander manner. Awe is enhanced. And you know a love that accepts you and your congregation in spite of your feeble efforts to save the liturgy with your *perfect* theological expressions. It is *strange how we say we cannot save ourselves and then act like we can save liturgy.*

When you think you have the know-how (the power) to create a liturgy that will keep God from being embarrassed, you have created an incongruity. The assumption that you can save God makes for a spirit that perverts the liturgy. While the liturgy may be theologically sound, this *hubris* spirit of the leader of worship creates the incongruity.

When you feel that your liturgy does God a favor, somebody is laughing at you. Or should be.

Liturgy is not a means by which you make God speak. Liturgy is a means by which God speaks to you.

C. *Liturgies must be adapted to the situation,* in keeping with where the congregation is at the time.

1. I have attended funeral services led by the best informed preachers, including bishops and seminary professors, and I have preached a few hundred funerals myself. I have seen the precise Order for the Burial of the Dead from the Book of Worship used very few times. When I read the Order in the Book of Worship, I think I know why it is not used so much in its present form. It comes off the paper as cold as death itself. The reason for this, as I see it, is that the one order presupposes universal application. And that just cannot be. *Each funeral service is different.*

In one of my pastorates a man died who had been an officer and a teacher of the Men's Bible Class, Finance Committee Chairman, Administrative Board Chairman, usher—you name it—and he had done it through the church. I never had so many calls telling me how fine a man this one was that we were going to bury. This called for a worship service of celebration. I told how I did not have to preach his funeral. The man did it himself before he died. The liturgy on that day celebrated life. When the people left, they carried victory in their hearts. That same day, I received a telephone call from a member of my pastorate who comes to church one Sunday a year, and that is Easter. Every other Sunday he is fishing. Nobody has ever heard of his doing anything for anybody though as a successful businessman, he could. The man was sobbing over the phone. Between his sobs he said, "Bob, that was the most moving funeral service I ever heard. No matter where you are, when I die I want you to come and preach my funeral. And I want one just like you gave my friend today!"

At this point, I would like to offer not a universal ritual for the burial of the dead, but some universal criteria that will help you create each ritual as the situation demands:

(1) Know something about the dead person. Certainly know if the dead is male or female. I know one preacher who preached the entire funeral sermon for the husband, when all the time the husband was sitting in the front row. It was the wife who had died! They very nearly had to bury the preacher after that sad day.

(2) Counsel the family to close the casket before the worship service begins. No amount of planning, liturgy, nor preaching can overcome the problems encountered at open-casket funeral services. Incongruities have a way of coming at those times. One preacher I know buried a man who never got along with his second wife. The preacher told me how he was called to their home during an argument. He knew something was wrong when he arrived. The wife was reading the Bible, and the husband was in the back yard washing the car. These were the very things the two never did in their more normal times. At the funeral were the deceased man's children by his first wife, his now-widowed second wife, and her children by her first husband. These two clans met at the

open casket at the end of the service. They stood there for a few moments. Then she looked up at my preacher friend and said, "Brother Lee, he didn't make it. He didn't make it!"

"Those comments kind of hurt the man's children by his first wife," Bro. Lee said to me, and continued, "Some of them had hopes that he did make it!"

(3) Be alert to personal comments by close members of the family. Use those comments in your sermon. And above all speak to the family. In that situation people are not gathered to hear you read a ritual. If you do read a ritual, read it *to the family*. Pick out appropriate scriptures, and read (or quote) them *to the family*. Be God's spokesman *to the family*. Whatever hymns are played or sung, let them be hymns that speak *to the family*.

This is not the time to try to convert the world, or to judge the deceased into or out of Heaven. It is a time to bring strength *to the family*.

2. Books have been written on what goes into the order for *the Sacrament of Holy Communion*. This book deals with *incongruities* that *break into the order*.

There are those who get more out of Communion than was ever intended to be in there. Those moments furnish incongruities that make for humor. At one of our larger East Texas United Methodist churches there is a round brass rail slightly above the kneeling area, and below the area where the small cups of juice are placed. When the mother and father came down with their two pre-school age sons, the two lads positioned themselves far enough away from the parents' control to pull off this typical cowboy-at-the-bar routine. They each took the small cup, put a foot on the brass rail, up went the cup of juice as the head went back, and in an audible "swigging" manner they ended their "communion" with an "ahhhhh!"

The parents saw it; the preacher saw it; the congregation heard it. And muffled laughter prevailed for a few moments.

Wisely the preacher never let on that anything out of the ordinary occurred. Later, however, he let out the laughter he contained when the parents stayed to apologize for this new interpretation of the liturgy for Holy Communion.

This was another one of those times when Truth, in illumining the incongruity, revealed the Real Presence of God in Holy Communion, even when all did not come off to human eyes and ears as Holy. God's Grace is there beyond man's most ludicrous ways.

3. We are taught (as we should be) to be worshipful during wedding ceremonies. All plans are designed with that purpose in mind. But *on the day of the wedding, incongruities pop at you* from every angle. I recall one wedding where the only things congruent were the incongruities. Everything seemed to go wrong. In the first place the bride was fifteen minutes late for her wedding. After the parents of the bride and groom were seated, the singer began to sing—at the same time the ushers rolled out the white runner down the center aisle (this innovation was supposed to have been done before she sang). The white runner down the aisle looked pretty, but wrinkled into large folds as the groomsmen met the bridesmaids at the front and center of the church to lead them to their places at the altar. Each time one of the groomsmen would twist the runner the groom, with body from waist up straight as a board, would reach out with his left foot and peck the runner back into place in a most unassuming manner. It took an average of six stabs at the runner for each of the five groomsmen. I counted. By the time the bride was ready to walk down, the groom had completed a leg exercise program.

As the minister whom I was assisting and I stood before the congregation, it was assigned to me as host pastor to give the mother of the bride the sign when it was time for her to stand to receive the bride coming down the aisle. Her standing in turn was the signal for the people to stand. Just then, I saw the photographer coming down the side aisle to take a picture of the bride from the front of the church. (Our printed rules state specifically this is not to be done. And this man knew that since he had photographed weddings in our church many times.) At the precise moment that I was to signal with my head for the bride's mother to stand, I was shaking my head ever so slightly for the photographer *not* to come down. He saw me, and grinned like the Devil that was in him at the time. I was not grinning. It was for a few seconds a stand-off. And then he relented and walked back to the narthex. By that time half the congregation was standing and waiting for the bride to come down. And the mother of the bride was too. I was limp from the anxiety of the moment just passed.

And then when the visiting minister read the vows, the Best Man brought out of his pocket a ring of keys that fitted every lock in the county. But there was no ring. He retrieved the ring finally from the other pocket.

During the proceedings someone passed a hankie via three bridesmaids to the teary-eyed bride. In spite of much of the proceedings, for her it was a moving experience.

And wouldn't you know it? At the conclusion of the ceremony, the usher came first for the parents of the groom!

D. *"When two or more gather in my name, I will be there."* [75] Whatever those two or more say or do "in His name" is an order of worship. In some congregations this is a hymn, a prayer, and a sermon. In other congregations the order may be organ prelude, choral call to worship, processional, hymn of praise, Prayer of Confession, Prayer of Intercession, Prayer of Petition, Responsive Reading, Words of Assurance, Gloria Patri, Glimpses of Church life, Offertory Prayer, Doxology, Hymn of Love, Scripture Reading, Pastoral Prayer, Choir Anthem, Hymn of Commitment, and a sermonette if there is time for it! In both of these orders of worship (and all shades between), the order is a vital part of worship if, for that congregation, it is a means to worship God. The moment the order of worship becomes an end in itself, the practice becomes *liturgiolatry—a worship of liturgy.* You can see this taking place today in large cathedrals with few in attendance. The liturgy includes every imaginable relational "dialogue" with God. The few in the congregation leave saying things like, "wasn't *that* beautiful!" and "I love *that* ritual." They have worshipped the liturgy and when this worship of liturgy is passed off as if it is worship of God, it is ludicrous.

1. Whatever liturgy is used fulfills its purpose if it is a means whereby you worship God. If liturgy does that for a congregation, it works. And *if it works, do not fix it!* A leader of worship borders on liturgiolatry when he/she tries to standardize his/her liturgy in every local church. This approach does not take into account where each congregation is in its understanding of the use of liturgy. I am reminded of the young seminary graduate who went into his first church, a small rural church, with his bulletin printed for an organ prelude. The problem was: they did not have an organ, only a piano with no piano player. He had printed "choir processional," but there was no choir. He did not know what to do. So he did what he could. He just put the ritual aside and tried to preach. That was perfectly all right with the small congregation. That was what they were used to anyway!

The liturgist who puts the mechanics of worship in the place of the experience of worship never quite gets things as they *ought to be.* About the time he gets all the symbolism to fit his personal theology of worship, he moves. Another liturgist comes in and says, "Uh, uh, that's not the way to do it. That's inconsistent with what happens in worship." The truth is: you never get everything consistent in the thinking of all

102

the people who walk into the sanctuary, or auditorium, or whatever you call the place where you go in and worship God. Somebody will come in and spot an incongruity that you do not see (and will not if you do not want to!). For instance, I went to a church once where the choir sang from the balcony in the back of the church. The reason for that arrangement: The choir is to be heard, not seen. That sounded logical enough for me. Then after many Sundays there I noticed the choir was robed. So I asked the chairman of the Worship Committee why the choir wore robes. He answered: "That's so that all the different colors and styles of dresses, suits, etc. cannot be seen." The choir that sat in the balcony in order not to be seen wore robes in order that their mixed dress would not be seen. Since I, from the pulpit, was the only one who could see them, I assumed they robed in order that their street clothes did not distract me. But then, when they were seated, I could hardly see the robes at all.

In order to let the congregation know that the choir was not distracting me by displaying an array of dress that bothered me, I had the choir come down to the front periodically and sing. That seemed to satisfy the need for consistency in the mind of the preacher!

2. It is easier for a congregation to accept a *change in liturgy* if it *is done slowly, and made meaningful by the worship leader.* This is the key to any use of liturgy. The worship leader must be comfortable with the liturgy, making every part an expression of his/her own deep understanding of what it means to worship God. If the leader merely acts like he/she is "into" the worship, the congregation will see through the facade. And they will find it extremely difficult to worship under those circumstances. If he/she does not feel deeply what he/she is doing with the liturgy, the congregation will feel somewhat the same way. If a part of the liturgy means something to you, use it. If it does not, do not. If the

liturgy means something to you, it can mean something to the worshipper (but will not if you pay no attention to others' desires). I am reminded of the preacher who announced to his people, "This is what I was told to do in Seminary." Right off many in the congregation saw that he did not know any more of what was going on than they did, and from then on it was every worshipper for him/herself.

3. *Liturgiolatry happens when you try to make every part fit your image of what ought to be,* rather than let it be an expression of who you are in the Presence of God. You do not allow room for sneezes, a questioning child, a blackout. I know a preacher who could hardly carry on the service of worship after the altar candles went out. One went, and all eyes went to the one candle that faltered, flickered, and finally flitted out. The lights symbolized God's Presence. But by the manner in which the preacher acted, you would think that God could not function at all without the candles burning. The preacher could not function! In that moment people began to smile at the whole affair. The incongruity had been illumined by Truth—the Presence of God! God was in the humor as surely as He was in the sublime.

When you plan your liturgy, keep in mind that finite, fallible, incongruent creatures plan liturgy, and use it. When something does go wrong—in spite of your best plans—you will go the right way in handling a bungling error. You will react with a sense of humor, laugh at the incongruity, and go on in your response to the Presence of God. Humor becomes one of many ways that you affirm the Presence of God in worship.

With a sense of the incongruities in all of life, you will not be shocked out of your wits when a problem disrupts your liturgy. When a power outage occurs and the lights go out and the organ stops playing, God is there and turns the intrusion into humor. The leader of worship can in one breath recognize the humor, and turn the minds of the worshippers back to God (whose Truth illuminated the incongruity) by saying something like, "Let us now do what the New Testament church did when they had a power outage. Let's pray." A short prayer for God's continued Presence would be in order. This lets the audience know that God is there when things go wrong in worship just as He is there when things go wrong in life.

4. *Humor is never planned into the liturgy.* Liturgy is no place for planned humor. For the worship leader and the worshipper any humor must come from a "natural" incongruity where both the leader and the congregation fall under Truth that illumines all incongruities. If the congregation sensed that the worship leader was revealing just their incongruities, it would not be funny to them. It would be a put-down of them. That effort would alienate them from God (and from the leader!), rather than permit them to sense His Presence.

You do not have to plan humor to have humor in the liturgy. Incongruities will be there because people are there. People are filled with incongruities no matter where they are; and that includes worship. It took no planning for humor that day when the preacher in the midst of worship uncovered the sacrament of the Lord's Supper, and found no elements. He knew that the elements were supposed to be there. He had put them there himself. What he did not know was that his small son had come along behind him and eaten the bread and drank the wine. The Lord's Supper abruptly ended. But once God's Truth illumined the total situation, redemption came through the humor and left the congregation with an unique awareness of God's Presence. That was one Communion service they would never forget. Somehow the absence of the elements dramatically made them realize how needed is the body and blood of Jesus Christ in this life they now live. Finally, that spontaneous incongruity, that unplanned part of the liturgy (it was part of the acted-out existential liturgy), turned out to be the most meaningful part of the service.

Every worship leader remembers those times that Truth came to the congregation stronger in the unplanned incongruities than in the planned liturgy. I remember the time I was baptizing a baby. We were well into the liturgy for the baptismal service when the baby's four-year-old sister, who was standing beside her parents during the baptismal service, began to show some discomfort with the situation (the baby had earlier whimpered a bit as I took her from the parents and handed her back to them). I stopped all proceedings and bent over and said to the four-year-old: "Is something troubling you?" I should not have said this. The child looked up at me, and with a frown on her face said loud enough for all to hear, "My little sister does not like to be passed around to everybody everywhere." The congregation broke into laughter. Somehow we went on with the worship service. You would think that something like that would disrupt a service beyond recovery. Not so. God through His illuminating Truth used that moment of humor to speak in a manner He had not before. That afternoon one of the members of that congregation called and said to me: "I do not remember the hymns sung. I don't remember what you preached. But I will never forget what happened during that infant baptismal service." The lady continued, "When you stopped in the middle of that service, when the whole congregation stopped and gave attention to that one little child, it made me realize, like never before, how God gives every one of us His undivided attention." That unplanned humor in liturgy was a medium of God's Truth for the lady, for the whole congregation, and for me, the one who was "passing the little sister around to everybody everywhere."

Any God-centered event in a worship service is liturgy. If it is a devotional only, that one event is liturgy. For those congregations who have few parts in their liturgy, the temptation toward liturgiolatry—toward worshiping the liturgy rather than allowing that mini-structured liturgy to be a means of true worship of God—is just as great as those involved in liturgiolatry who put into the liturgy every conceivable interaction between God and man. The same pride works on both liturgists. When the I-am-right-and-you-are-wrong attitude possesses a liturgist at either extreme (or anywhere in between), you have the practice of liturgiolatry. You have seen how this pride entraps the "high-church" liturgist and makes for incongruities in him/her. He/she is acting like what he/she is not. No human can be *that* right. That same incongruity may be seen in the "low church" liturgist who proclaims his/her *right* liturgy with button-bustin' pride, "*We* don't even have a liturgy. *We* just preach Jesus Christ!" When people say this, you do not see nor hear a witness for Christ so much as you see and hear an expression of someone whose *hubris* has lofted her/himself to the land of the gods. He is still a mere mortal. The gap between that fact and where she/he thinks she/he is triggers the humor.

E. *Some parts of liturgy are always being debated.* Should they or should they not be included? My answer is: They *may* be included if they point toward God, but do not necessarily *have to be* included. This could apply to the "Call To Worship"; it could apply to the "Children's Sermon." Since the "Children's Sermon" is more controversial than the "Call To Worship," let us look at that innovative entree into worship. Does it *primarily* reveal spiritual interplay between the congregation and God, or is it *primarily* a performance for the audience to enjoy? The identifying word in this instance is *primarily*. Liturgy may be *primarily* God-centered, and consequently be entertaining because of incongruities. But if it is *primarily* entertaining, it is not God-centered, but man-centered. Some simply enjoy watching their children perform as they congregate before the preacher. This interpretation is more child-centered than God-centered. Others seem to understand and learn from that sermon far better than the highly intellectual "adult" sermon that comes later. That interpretation may be more God-centered than the "adult" sermon because the congregation understands that sermon. If the preacher would simply substitute that children's sermon for the adult sermon, then there would be no need for the children's sermon. And most (not all!) would know what the preacher said.

But then there are good children's sermons, and bad children's sermons. Some simply are not sermons. In a petty moralistic fashion they say, "Be good boys and girls so that God will love you."

And then there is the parent who pushes her child to go down to the front. Older children often rebel, but do finally go down for this embarrassing manipulation by the preacher for the entertainment of the adults.

God's Truth shines in spite of those man-centered circumstances—through humor. When these performances are passed off as liturgy, the result is more ludicrous than worshipful. That ludicrous revelation is seen in this story told by the late Jim Clelland, dean of Duke Chapel:

A preacher opened his children's sermon with this question to the boys and girls, "Children, what has a bushy tail, eats nuts and lives in a tree?"

An eight-year-old boy answered, "God."

The congregation erupted into laughter, and the children's sermon came to an abrupt end.

After the service, as the congregation filed out, the preacher took the boy aside and asked, "Look, kid, what did you mean by answering 'God' when I asked that question in the sermon? Didn't you know I was talking about a squirrel?"

"Sure I knew you were talking about squirrels. But you're a preacher, aren't you? This is a church, and you're supposed to be talking about God, not squirrels!"

God's Truth illumined the ontic incongruity: trying to make what *was not* (the squirrel) look as it *ought to be* (God). That revelation of Truth through the incongruity, through the laughter, brought God to the congregation whether they realized it or not. Because of His Truth, God cannot fail to come through. Even when the congregation fails to worship God, God does not fail the congregation.

1. *Who is to judge which parts of the ritual are man-centered,* and which parts are God-centered? Who says that the prayer of confession is man-centered or God-centered? Or the Doxology? Or the Offertory? The judgment rests with the congregation. What is God-centered with one congregation may not be with another congregation. For instance, the movements and impressions of interpretive dance during a worship service could conceivably stir within a worshipper a deep thirst for God. For others such movements would be absolutely repulsive. For this reason the interpretive religious dance has not been universally accepted as part of liturgy. As one fellow put it: "They might have 'danced before the Lord' in the Bible, but here they 'danced before the people,' and the people did not care for it. We had just as soon they 'dance before the Lord' some place else." The liturgy is to guide the people as they worship God. If the people as a whole (there is always someone who will not like something about the particular liturgy) are repulsed by a part of the liturgy, that part should be deleted—no matter how theologically sound it is to the worship leader. It is not theologically sound in the minds of the congregation, or they would not feel the way they do. How does a worship leader deal

with this lack of understanding on the part of a congregation? He/she can accept the truth that no Truth (as theologically sound as all truth is!) can be force-fed into a congregation.

When a worship leader refuses to accept this, he/she sets up incongruities in the worship service that make for unintended humor. I remember the time a balding campus chaplain on one of our Methodist university campuses was caught by the camera in the act of dancing in his clerical robe down the aisle of the campus chapel with a lovely young co-ed clad in tight "hot pants." Those present saw the event in different ways. Some said the dance down the aisle was absolutely angelic. Others said the two had their timing off in spite of intense preparation for this act of worship. Still others admitted they did not know what was going on, but it was exciting. And that was more than they could say about some worship services in the chapel. At this sight nearly everybody laughed. Some even clapped.

For the hundreds of thousands who were not there, and saw the picture, there were mixed emotions and many laughs—and many letters to the Dean, as well as cancelled pledges to the school.

The chaplain gave his reasons for making this dance down the aisle with the hot-panted co-ed. And in his thinking they were theologically sound. For many his theological *thinking* was no problem. It was his acting it out that bothered them!

Some might say, "But he was the worship *leader*. It was his responsibility to lead out in these areas of experimental worship." And that is a true statement. But a worship leader is not a worship *shocker*. Any time you inject shock treatment into the liturgy, you invite the congregation's attention upon the act, and nothing else. Any event that shocks gains attention to itself. That is a part of the dynamics that go with shock treatment.

2. And again, *the worship leader is not known as the wor-*

ship experimenter. He/she leads. And if he/she experiments at all, it is not for experiment's sake, but a different way of expressing the same attitudes of the heart toward God in worship. A worship leader never experiments with worship in the same manner a scientist experiments in the laboratory. The scientist may play around with his experiments; the worship leader cannot play around with the things of God. And that includes liturgy. Laboratory experiments are man-controlled; worship is Grace-controlled. The worship leader may put something different in the liturgy. But he will not be doing it in a "playing around" manner.

3. There is *no order of worship for entertainment.* But worship should have its pleasant moments. If you want to call those pleasant high moments entertainment, fine, just so long as you, the worship leader, do not make pleasantness the goal of liturgy. That pleasant feeling may come from an anthem that stirs emotions. Ecstasy is a valid experience that comes in the moment of worship. It is when your notes say, "Be ecstatic here," that problems arise. That contrivance will be caught by Truth. The people will sense it. And the incongruity will evoke humor.

4. *A worship leader should be a good reader.* If you monotone along, the people hear your monotone more than they hear the text. If you read with a flair, they will note your flair more than they will hear the text. If you mispronounce a word, they will not hear another word you say. Those goofs account for many a glancing grin in the congregation. One of the first things a liturgist needs to learn to do is to read. If he/she does not, the unintended incongruities (he/she ought to know better, but does not) can overwhelm the liturgy to the point that the unintended liturgist/comic becomes the center of attention rather than God.

5. The moment he/she starts playing around with liturgy, you can be sure the ludicrous is about to follow. *Some groups have used liturgy to promote their own ideology.* This was the

case with a national church organization's use of the following litany:

SERVICE OF RE-COMMISSIONING AND COMMUNION
4-H CENTRE, WASHINGTON, D.C.
January 1974

Gathering as a Community

Informal Singing
The International Gathering

Minister: As we gather in this particular community to worship together, we are not alone. We gather in the fellowship of all those who have gone before us, who surround us in this moment, and speak to us out of eternity.

Minister: Those whose actions and power have shaped the course of human history, and those whose lives have been shaped by them;
—Peking man, Neanderthal man, and those nameless men and women who decided to be human beings, to create human life, to stand and walk, to use fire, and to have dominion over the earth;
—Alexander the Great, Constantine, Attila the Hun, the Caliphs of the Middle East, Sun Yatsen, Nehru, the Aztecs, Kwame Nkrumah.

People: Those who in the midst of the struggles of power around them, sought to discover and express new dimensions of humanness;
—Gautama, the Buddha
  —Mohammed, the Prophet
    —Confucius, the Teacher
      —Krishna, the Hindu
        —Abraham, the Patriarch
          —Peter and Paul, the missionaries

112

Minister: Those who in times of laxity and retreat, have sought to rediscover and renew the springs of faith and humanness;
—Amos
　—Gandhi
　　—Luther
　　　—Wesley
　　　　—Marx

The worshippers seemed to be into the litany until they came to the part, "Luther, Wesley, Marx——." Some seemed to say over again "Luther, Wesley, *Marx*——How on earth did an atheist get into this?" The ontic incongruity was obvious. Something was not as it ought to be, but was made to look like it. The mood of many went from puzzlement to consternation to humor. It was laughable that someone would attempt to worship God as he/she praised an atheist. Through that illumined liturgical incongruity the Truth of God came to some in the congregation. This ideologically oriented liturgical ploy worked only for those who believed it in the first place. Most of the worshippers never recognized the incongruity. As far as they were concerned, *Marx* could have been some little known Bible character. And you just do not want to question some things that might reveal you have not read your Bible as carefully as you should. The majority of the people worshipped in spite of the liturgy. They had come from far and wide to this important meeting. For them God had to be there. And He was—in their hearts. And He revealed Himself to others through unintended incongruities. These intended uses of divinely oriented liturgy by an ideologically oriented "worship leader" finally created another incongruity that backfired on the "worship leader": what he/she assumed had happened had not happened. The joke was on them. Those who see the incongruity laugh at the absurdity of such a ritual.

6. Why is it that the use of a mini-orchestra stirs the souls

for a season? The congregation seems to appreciate the extra music. But what was once innovative to them no longer is. They come to expect it, but not expect it to do for their worship what it once did.

I would suggest that the answer to all these questions is ontological. *Men struggle for congruity.* Modern studies in communications theory support this conclusion. "So nature abhors inconsistency. In the realm of self-orientation, this rarely, if ever, entails a psychological state devoid of tension or conflict." [76]

Humor is a way that you can handle an incongruity. Humor remains a way that you can live in incongruent conditions and maintain a sense of congruity. The underlying purpose of the laugh, or exhilaration in the case of the worship service where a slight surprise incongruity is injected via music, self-devised litany, etc., is to return the occasion to a congruity, a consistency. A congregation's need of consistency is torn to shreds when too much of any good thing is put into the liturgy.

An innovation that remains in the liturgy soon loses its innovative mystique because it has now become a part of the consistency pattern. In a sense, the congregation appreciates more the now accustomed-to "innovation" because it fits their much-needed consistency pattern. This consistency pattern is maintained in some sub-culture congregations by a regular changing of the liturgy. They consistently expect a change. They consistently expect the incongruity. They celebrate change.

The ontological drive for consistency (that something be as it seems to be) is inherent in man's being. That's who he *is.* Thus it is not to man's blame nor credit that he is consistent in his worship. The question for man to ask is: consistent for what purpose? If it is to glorify God, it is worship. If it is to glorify self, it is liturgiolatry. In all kinds of idolatry man's prowess is elevated. That includes his efforts to show off during worship through his use of liturgy. Trying to make that show-off of self look like worship of God is ludicrous.

If change becomes the end purpose of liturgy, it is liturgiolatry. It becomes a constant experimentation for experimentation's sake. It may be an exciting, cheerful, and highly charged atmosphere, yet meaningless insofar as God is concerned. Man's effort to make *change* look like God is ludicrous, ludicrous because he tries to make what is not look like what *is*.

7. *Many feel that modern expressions of freedom must find their way into the liturgies* of worship services. This seems sensible enough. God is for freedom. If God is for it, so should we be for it. But is what we call freedom truly freedom? Or is it license that we have invited into liturgy? In the name of freedom our liturgies tend to accommodate any thought or action. You must be open to whatever celebration people want, or you will be against freedom. You cannot draw the line anywhere if you are for freedom. That rationale drove one local church to celebrate human sexuality by allowing a female member of the congregation to stand before the congregation and undress. The people celebrated with shouts of "Amen!" "Praise the Lord," hand clapping, laughing, etc. The writer who wrote about this said it was quite a celebration.

His use of the word *celebration* reminds me of a book on liturgy where not once was the word *worship* used. On every page the word used to picture what happens in a church service was *celebration.* Which leads me to say: all worship is a celebration, but not every celebration is worship.

When you celebrate license as if it were liberty, the incongruity is ludicrous. For instance, any man in that congregation who, in viewing the naked lady, said he was thinking of God, celebrates the lie as if it were truth. And the affair is as comic as it is tragic.

In all of life there is humor in man's struggles for freedom.

115

And when we know the Truth, we know the power that spotlights the gaps and elicits the humor. Only in a state of freedom, then, can we see the humor. A free spirit senses incongruities. When we are imprisoned within our own selves, we see life "straight." When we are free under God's Truth, we can see incongruities, ours as well as others. This new-found freedom does not give serenity and protection from every disturbance. Quite the contrary, awareness of a magnitude undreamed comes with this freedom.[77]

In all of life there is humor in man's struggles for freedom. And that includes his struggles for freedom in liturgy.

Unintended humor in worship could be lessened considerably if the following instructions were followed: "Until one has probed deeply in this area he has no more business trying out new forms of worship than he has taking unlabeled medicines. Essentially the theological norm is the investigation of any act of worship as to its adequacy in reflecting Christian faith." [78]

F. You have seen where planned humor is appropriate in sermons. *There is no place for intended humor in the order of worship.* The reason for this is: you are doing your best to express praise, worded adoration, and thanksgiving to God. And that is serious business. But the unintended humor has a way of getting into the act of worship. It is this unintended humor, when we act like what we are not and do not know it, that this Part IV points out. These incongruities show up in spite of our best intentions.

When you recognize incongruities in the order of worship, the humor is inevitable. Since the incongruity was illumined by Truth, it is God-given. You should thank God for the insight. But you should not plan to use that laugh in a later order of worship. To use that laugh would draw attention to yourself and not to God, and would thus rob you of the meaning of worship. When something comic happens in the order of worship, you may or may not laugh. You definitely would not plan such an event into a worship service.

1. *A sense of humor can keep the sublimeness* of the worship occasion when an incongruity suddenly comes from nowhere. An honest recognition of the incongruity releases the congregation to laugh, and allows them to move on with the order of worship.

You do not plan for humor in the worship service. It has a way of coming of its own accord. Humans can make mistakes any time anywhere. That includes the worship service. And the human in that situation may be the leader of worship. A good sense of humor has proved to be one of the best ways of handling human bungling in those times. One of the most delightful persons I know is Mrs. Hallie Morton, noted United Methodist Church leader in the Texas Conference. Her serious involvement in Christian mission, coupled with a not-so-serious look at herself, allows God to save the occasion when mistakes are made. One such occasion was a worship service in which she was the leader in worship. She had lost her place in the hymnal at the time she was supposed to be leading the Responsive Reading. She stood at the lectern, not knowing what to do. She could not find the number in the bulletin. It was there. But she still could not see it. Finally a man from the congregation said, "Hallie, it's your time now."

She answered, "I know it is Jim, but where am I?"

On those days when everything goes wrong, they seem to go wrong worse during a worship service. I hope I never again see a day like this one I am about to describe. The first service went fine. And then everything fell apart. The collection plates had not been returned to the sanctuary after the first service. Have you ever tried to take up an offering without the plates?

When a couple joined our church that day, the associate

minister in charge of evangelism gave me a card with their names on it. I introduced the new couple to the congregation, and said, "Get to know these new members, and show them you care." About that time the associate minister was making his way over to me. He whispered, "I made a mistake. I gave you the wrong names." And then he told me their names. But I was not sure whether he was changing their first names or last names. Till this day I am not sure what name I used to introduce them to the congregation. I did not even know the name of the people I had just admonished the congregation to get to know!

That evening we celebrated Holy Communion. In the middle of the service I realized not enough elements had been prepared. Have you ever given the dismissal prayer to communicants who never even saw the elements?

When we got home that night, my wife Doris said to me, "This has been a long day, hasn't it?"

I answered, "You will never know how long, my dear, you'll never know how long!"

What do you do when everything seems to come apart at the seams and mistakes are made? When imperfect people act perfect anywhere, including worship, you have a laughable situation. Regardless how you react in that ludicrous moment, you have a laughable situation. God's Truth has illumined another incongruity. But this does not mean you necessarily have to laugh out about the fiasco. At the same time that Truth illumines the incongruity, it also illumines beyond the incongruity to the congruent occasion and says, "Don't turn this into a comedy." In that case you may or may not recognize the incongruity with a laugh—so long as you do not lose the transcending Purpose that calls you in worship. Sometimes a recognition of the incongruity that releases the laugh pent up in the congregation helps turn the attention of the worshippers back to God—to the same Truth that revealed the ludicrous. Sometimes it does not. I believe

118

that Truth will "tell" you when to, and when not to, laugh. For instance, on that day when I had no collection plates, I opted not to recognize the incongruity of having to take up an offering with no offering plates. The congregation noticed the mistake, and could have laughed; but did not. The ushers covered my mistake when they garnered from somewhere extra offering plates. In the moment the blunder, I felt, was not big enough in the congregation's mind for me to recognize the incongruity with a statement that spotlighted the mistake. And later in the worship service when I read the wrong names of the new members to the congregation, and the associate minister whispered to me that he had made a mistake and gave me the wrong names, the blunder was too big in the eyes of the congregation to overlook. I told the people about the wrong name given me. And then remarked to the associate (but in reality was speaking to the congregation), "Well, that's just the second mistake we've ever made, and that's not so bad." The people laughed off the tension. The associate in a pale whiteness laughed, even more nervously. But he laughed at himself. And I laughed at myself. And that helped. When you blunder, if you can laugh at yourself, it always helps. I never did make the proper announcement of the new members. But you can cover just so many goofs, and it is time to go on.

That evening, when the mistake was made concerning the placing of the elements of Holy Communion, the first group had come and gone from the altar before I realized that over half of them did not receive the elements. The goof was obvious, but this was not the time to laugh because the transcending Truth of God's Presence in Holy Communion, admittedly the same Truth that illumined the incongruity, said to the communicants that He was there "in" the elements that they received in their hearts, but never saw nor touched. They had communion in their hearts without the elements in their stomachs. In some ways that was for some as Holy a

Communion, as sublime as any they ever "took." While the incongruity was present, God voided that revelation of an incongruity, and presented His Being-there as the main thrust of His Truth. You never laugh at the things of God. Only with Him, with His guidance, can you laugh the good laugh—can you have a true sense of humor.

2. Orders of worship are created to get and keep the attention of the gathered people. One problem is that *some people come to worship services expecting to be distracted.* This was the case with some people who attended worship services in a local theater while the new sanctuary was being built. A portable pulpit was set up. A piano was rolled in. Hymn books were passed out at the beginning of the services and picked up at the end. They managed with most of the surroundings very well. But they could not handle the frescos of nude women on the walls. The dim lighting did not shade the frescos as much as it did the glimpses, and sometimes the glaring stares of some in the congregation. Records show that attendance actually grew under these circumstances. The preacher felt he was the reason until they moved into their new facility and the crowds dropped off. Then he realized he had some help in the theater. And it was not all divine!

The best order of worship does little to get the attention of someone who is determined to be distracted anyway. I shall never forget the man who said: "Those kids in the balcony keep talking and disturbing my worship." I suggested he move down to the lower floor where "those kids" would not bother him. He did this for a Sunday or two, and then moved back up to the balcony. Thinking that things were all right in the balcony again, I said to him, "I see you are back in the balcony. Is everything all right now?"

"No!" he said, "But I was there before those kids were. Let them move!"

He actually chose to be distracted. No kind of order of worship could get his attention.

Some unwittingly choose to be distracted. If you are not prepared for worship, the order of worship does little to help. I once had a choir director who asked for his music stand to be in a certain place. The custodian forgot to do it. Under his breath the choir director said, "That makes me so d——— mad."

That madness entered the sanctuary, and stayed there while he led the congregation in the hymn "Sweet Hour of Prayer."

3. *An order of worship keeps the experience from being a staged religious performance.* Every aspect of any order of worship is God-oriented. Without this, the service of "worship" becomes an ego input into a talent show where God is talked about. When that show is passed off as "worship," it is ludicrous. Such shows-on-the-road attract crowds as they make their way across the country. I will share with you a few of these I have read about, and some I have seen and heard until my hearing almost left me!

Have you listened to a religious rock concert? I have. And for our young folks' sakes (and for the sakes of those older folks whose hearing is gone anyway), I will have that show back in my pastorate some day. The leader of the religious rock group *said,* "This program glorifies God." And immediately they went into the act. He called on a lovely girl to quote spontaneously a scripture. "Without giving a thought just speak it out," he said. Quicker than the snap of a finger, she "spontaneously" quoted a verse from Philippians, just as she had done a hundred times. The unintended incongruity stood out boldly. Nobody laughed. But there was in some of us a grin on the inside. Throughout the so-called "service to praise God" they did monkeyshines, like featuring some of the musicians in comic routines. Some seemed to make the instruments "talk." The drummer made his music "dance." After each performance, the audience clapped, just like they are supposed to do following fine entertainment. Between songs the leader preached, "Now, I'm not a preacher, etc., etc.," as he modulated his voice from a whisper to a shout. It was a fine evening's entertainment that one member called "lightning and thunder." It was fun as far as entertainment goes; it was *funny* when they tried to make it look like worship.

I have read newspaper accounts of a church that proudly proclaims it is "non-liturgical." It is that. Over and over they import entertainers to preach the "power of God." I remember the time they had a preacher parachute from a plane onto the church parking lot. I do not know what he said in his sermon that day, but he surely must have had a hard time explaining a sprained ankle as the result of the power of God. And then they advertised the world's yo-yo champion. The children gawked as the yo-yo yo-yoed across the floor, up, down, out, back. It climbed the string—slowly—fast. You ask the children what he said, and they cannot tell you. Ask them what he did, and they will say, "He yo-yoed." The latest venture I read about was a newspaper reporter's account of a karate expert's sermon on "the power of God." The pin-cushion preacher allowed his torso to be sandwiched between two beds of nails. A half-ton block of concrete was put on top of that. To prepare himself for this show of strength, he paced across the stage, growling and grunting to work up adrenaline. As he peaked out, he smashed seven stacked concrete slabs with a forearm. He was now ready. He lay upon the bed of nails. In a matter of a few seconds, volunteers had placed the second bed on his chest. A layman smashed it with a sledge hammer. They pulled the preacher out of the rubble. After this exhibition, he revealed fifteen nail cuts on his right side. At another church he received thirty nail cuts when some of the people assigned to lift the block off him went into shock and did not get the weight off him. Some of the people truly believe in *him*. The service that night ended with his splitting with a Samurai sword a potato perched on the head of one of the deacons. The whole crowd almost went into shock. The service ended, not with an "Amen," but with a prolonged "wheeuuuuu!"

4. It does not take a great theological mind to know what to do in a worship service. *A little common sense thinking will go a long way.*

Truth cannot be laughed *at* because it is of God. It *is*. The congruent quality of Truth illumines incongruities. The sense in man that recognizes incongruities under Truth's illumination is called *common* sense, not a philosophical sense as is written in this paragraph, not in the sense of logic, but in common sense. Common sense functions best in your mind when your mind is off yourself. This makes common sense one of the most uncommon experiences of the human mind. Truth again is the key to the workings of common sense. Common sense senses Truth. It senses that you talk too much about yourself while you have acted humble in the process, and permits you to laugh at yourself. The more your mind is on yourself, the more ludicrous will be your actions. You think too much about your *self* in what you are thinking rather than about *what* you are thinking. That sets the stage for ludicrous actions.

Common sense is a givenness rather than an accomplishment. It works easier when man's mind is in neutral, rather than when the mind runs in high gear, blurting out whatever it thinks, or in a low-geared deliberate manner that pulls hard at every thought. This *givenness* functions better when the mind/heart thinks/feels the Truth. That desire to be truthful permits common sense to sense incongruities, to help people laugh, and to act spontaneously in a manner that is palatable to all concerned.

Having a sense of humor is not the same as being funny all the time. Having a sense of humor means seeing the incongruity, but having sense enough not to laugh if the situation is too close to the tragic dimensions of the comic/tragic situation. A sense of humor includes the sense to know which interpretation is called for in the moment. One day you may laugh; another day you may not. Only this extra sense, that comes with a sense of humor, can "tell" you that. I believe that extra sense comes with the Truth from God that not only illumines the incongruity, but "tells" you when to and when not to laugh about it.

If you see the incongruity, and the congregation does not, do not tell them about it. In the first place, if you have to tell them, it is no incongruity for them. And your explaining the incongruity destroys the humor.

> Humor reacts to incongruities within the ambiguities of life. Humor leaves when the incongruities are seen in the raw, when they are intellectualized in this ontology. But humor, a divine gift to see with truth incongruities, comes again through the next laugh, when we are again surprised by our glimpse of the "gap." When humor is evaluated, it no longer is laughable; a totally serious self is dealing with, of all things, the subject of humor.[79]

A worship leader with a sense of humor has sense enough not to use it. He knows the sublimeness of the occasion. He also knows he can recognize unintended incongruities that come—if the occasion warrants it.

A developed *sense* of humor remains the best means of handling incongruities that may crop up in the order of worship. You may know that you have grown in developing this sense of humor when you more keenly sense your own inherent incongruities. This is called sanctification.

> Progress toward spiritual maturity (sanctification) can be judged by our sense of humor. We stymie our progression when we will not choose in accordance with the Truth that reveals incongruities midst all the ambi-

124

guities. Maturity comes, not as an accomplishment of character, but as a keener awareness of what is going on in the world, and a willingness to accept one's world the way Truth reveals it. That is sanctification accomplished in freedom lived out, and lived out to a large extent in humor. For example, a Holy Joe acting like that, who sees, under Truth, the incongruity of not being what he acts like, will now *become* a mature Holy Joe because now he sees he is not what he acts like and laughs at his feeble efforts *to be*. That laugh with Truth is maturity in the making and makes a sense of humor a sure sign of sanctification.[80]

That awareness keeps you from taking your own self too seriously. There is nothing funnier than a worship leader who tries to look more holy than God as he/she parades through the liturgy. A congregation who senses that in their leader will never get into the liturgy. They are too busy watching a worship leader who is "too sincere" as he/she prays the Prayer of Confession, "too pious" as he/she receives God's forgiveness, "too bouncy" in the reading of the Responsive Reading, "too exuberant" as he/she praises God. When the worship leader takes himself/herself too seriously in his/her role, it simply becomes *too much* for the congregation. The leader has captured their attention by his/her incongruity. The congruity of the Power of God's Presence has been displaced by an incongruity in the being of the worship leader. This is at the same moment both tragic and comic.

While the tragic apprehension of the contradiction despairs of a way out, the comic interpretation cancels the contradiction and renders it less painful. This does not mean that the tragic apprehension is "bad." Tragic insight recognizes the good/evil ambiguities within the contradiction; the humorous reaction resolves the con-

125

tradiction without destroying the tragic insight. Because of this relatedness, humor may come in the worst forms of human sufferings.[81]

If you are that worship leader, and you see your own incongruities in these *Gawdly* actions (the people see you acting like what you *are not)*, a laugh at yourself will free you *to be* the kind of leader who will focus your attention more truly upon God in worship. When the congregation sees that taking place in you, they will likely follow.

5. In the sixties and far into the seventies, liturgists in zest for their cause over-reacted against "the preacher." They diminished the preacher image and opted for the liturgical leader image. They felt this better fitted the total experience of the worship service. In attempting to carry out what seemed to them a mandate from God, they attacked the preaching aspect of the worship service by describing it as "outdated," "overplayed," "nonsacramental," "noncommunicative," etc. Many preachers attempting to preach today went through seminary and never had a course in homiletics. They got out into the local churches and heard the laity say, "While you are here, you might as well preach!" This constant barrage of criticism toward preaching turned out to be sacerdotalism-in-reverse. In talking down preaching, it seemed that people talked more about it than ever. The time has come for us to talk about worship and how *important good preaching and liturgical leadership are on the part of the minister.* The minister proclaims God's Word through preaching and the order of worship. His/her sense of humor assures him/her that God's Truth is there illumining incongruities even while he/she proclaims God's sublime Word of Grace.

PART V

HUMOR IN PREPARING THE SERMON

HUMOR IN
PREPARING THE SERMON

A. *Lack of adequate sermon preparation may cause unintended humor.*

1. *A goof in an effort to be funny brings off embarrassed laughter.* Rather than appreciating the speaker's humor, the audience feels sorry for him. He tries to tell something funny, forgets his lines, or mixes them up. The punch line comes off scrambled. The audience laughs—*at* him! For example, say to your audience, "An Aggie once borrowed a chain saw from a neighbor. When he got through sawing his trees, he carried the chain saw back and said, 'I wore out my arm trying to get that saw through the tree.'

"The neighbor said, 'You must remember that the motor does the cutting, not you.'" And the audience may grin because they see that you think you told a joke.

A better plan would be: "An Aggie once borrowed a chain saw from a neighbor. When the Aggie returned the saw, he and the saw seemed a bit scuffed up. The fatigued Aggie said, 'That is the dullest saw I ever saw. I wore myself out trying to saw that tree.'

"The neighbor said, 'Well, I don't understand that. The last time I used it, it worked perfectly.' The neighbor pulled the rope on the chain saw. The engine went, 'pop! pop! pop!' The Aggie said, 'What's that!' "

The audience will laugh *with* you.

2. *A goof in a straight sermon makes for unintended humor.* The disparity is made more obvious in a *straight* sermon. Brother Caleb Lancaster was serious when he preached.

> In the Lauren County Baptist Association it was the custom to have fifth Saturday and fifth Sunday meetings, with preaching in the morning and afternoon and "dinner on the church grounds."
>
> Brother Caleb Lancaster, a sweet and noble old man of seventy years, always conducted what he called the devotional at ten A.M. each fifth Saturday. The program committee never put anybody except Brother Caleb on for the ten A.M. hour.
>
> Brother Caleb Lancaster would go to the pulpit stand, open the Bible, pull his octagon-shaped glasses far down on his nose, look out at the congregation over his glasses, and say: "Well, dear folks, what verse my eye lights on I talks on."
>
> One morning, his eye "lit upon" Isaiah, the eighth chapter. In the first verse were these words: "Moreover the Lord said unto me, Take thee a great roll, and write in it with a man's pen concerning Mahershalalhashbaz" (Isa. 8:1).
>
> Brother Lancaster let his eyes "light" several times upon the verse. Then he said, with a bit of confusion, "I ain't never met that brother, and I ain't gointer speak to him today."
>
> At another time, at the fifth Saturday morning meeting, his eyes "lit" upon 2 Samuel 21:20: "And there was yet a battle in Gath, where was a man of great stature, and that had on every hand six fingers, and on every

foot six toes, four and twenty in number; and he also was born to the giant."

His comments upon that verse were something like this: "That shorely was a big guy! And if he had five-finger gloves, they wouldn't help. And if he had ingrowing toenails, he must have suffered a lot. My wife suffered for days when she had just one ingrowing toenail."

While we were eating "dinner on the grounds" at the tables loaded with all sorts of foods, I said to this great old man: "Brother Lancaster, I am just a young sprout and you are a giant tree in God's forest, and maybe I should not say to you what I am going to say. But why don't you get you a subject and a text, and you could say some good things that would help folks? So, please, sir, quit getting up and saying that "the first verse your eye lights on you talks on."

Three months later, the fifth Saturday and Sunday meeting was held at the grand old Prospect Baptist Church. *Brother Lancaster* took his place before the Bible stand in the pulpit. He pulled his octagon spectacles far down on his nose, and said: "Well, dear folks! The last time I had this devotional Brother Lee over here (and he nodded his head toward me), he said I ought to quit getting up and telling you that the first verse my eye lights on, I talks on. So I got me a subject and a text. My subject is 'Christian Activity' and you can find my text in the first verse of chapter number five of Second Kings—'Naaman was a leper.' " He pronounced "leper" as though it was "leaper." And he proceeded to tell us that Naaman did not sit down when there was something to be done, but he LEAPED. He did not stroll around, but LEAPED. He did not walk slowly or just run, but he LEAPED. And he urged us to believe that

131

the churches needed "a mighty host of LEAPERS," not crawlers, not sitters, not strollers, not lame walkers—but LEAPERS.[82]

The only thing that could save a preacher in that situation would be for the audience to interpret scripture as does the preacher!

3. Without adequate preparation there is no telling what you may say. Here are some *comments heard in sermons that caused unintended humor.* The preacher at the lady's funeral said, "She [the deceased] was a school teacher. With the exception of Christian work, more good can be done there than in any profession." This implied she could not be a school teacher and do Christian work!

I was there when one preacher got carried away during his sermon. He said: "That's just a bunch of bull!" I was the preacher!

A common practice among some preachers is to sprinkle throughout the sermon: "Praise the Lord!" That expression must be carefully used by a preacher or it can lead to unintended humor. One radio preacher stumbled into this when he obviously got his feet tangled in his lapel microphone's trailing cord. He unwittingly said, "This crazy cord is going to cause me to fall and break my neck. Praise the Lord!"

The best planning does not guarantee a successful use of humor. It does make for better possibilities of success.

B. *Possibilities of success—that is the best you can hope for.* You risk failure every time you use humor in your preaching. If you do not use humor (and you have a sense for it), you fail to use your potential. Much thought must go into whether you do or do not use humor.

1. *Some attempts by preachers to tell something funny invite failure.* For instance, when you say, "Let me tell you something funny," you set yourself up for a possible failure. You have set the stage for something funny, and what you say

may not be funny at all. Just say what you think is funny (but do not say that you think it is), and let the audience decide whether it is. Simply say, "Let me tell you something that happened." If the audience catches the humor, fine. If they do not, nothing is lost. Their *straight* interpretation of what you thought was funny may be congruent with the facts. Maybe it was not funny! You can accept this because you did not set yourself up by telling them to look for something funny when it was not funny to them. If after you tell your audience, "This story is going to be funny," somebody says, "That was funny," you just laid an ostrich egg!

If you tell the audience something is funny and it is not, you set yourself up to be laughed *at*. And that is not the kind of humor you want.

Distinguish between telling something that is funny and telling your audience that something is funny when it is not funny to them. Maybe they are too close to the situation for anything funny to be seen. For instance, you would not in the heat of the debate say to a congregation split over whether or not to put a fence around a playground on church property: "This whole affair is ludicrous." Do that and you can be sure to have both sides agreeing to attack *you!* The situation may be ludicrous to those removed far enough from the fray, but not to those who have their swords drawn. (Usually "swords" in church battles are Bibles! Each person quotes his verse to prove a *point*.) Again, tell something funny, but do not tell your audience something is funny when in their minds it may be a life-and-death matter.

2. *A "groaner" is a sure failure for a preacher.* A stand-up comic can use a "groaner" because he can use the audience's negative reaction to get a laugh. When Johnny Carson tells a story that causes the audience to groan, he begins to back up on the stage (as if the audience were going to attack him). *That* routine gets the healthy laugh he looks for. There is no reason for the preacher to use a "groaner." He is not on a

stage, trying to find a way to get a laugh. His purpose is to speak the Truth, and to see with the Truth the humor that comes through human incongruities. The ultimate purpose of his humor is not merely to entertain, but to speak the Truth.

Here are some preachers' "groaners" that audiences do not need to hear: "She asked me if I were a right-winger. I told her, 'No. I'm left-handed.' "

"He asked me if I were Orthodox. I said, 'No, my name is Bob Parrott.' "

O-o-o-o-o! I groan as I write these. You groan as you read them. Audiences groan when they hear them. So much for "groaners." They serve no useful purpose in preaching.

> . . . the habit of putting an obvious twist on words soon ceases to be funny. Wisecracking can become an affliction. Hectic facetiousness is not real humor. Ecclesiastes 7:6 describes it perfectly: "As the crackling of thorns under a pot, so is the laughter of the fools." [83]

C. Based on the insights of Part I of this book, here are *some guidelines to keep in mind when planning the sermon:*

1. *Since humor interprets tragedy, a misuse of that humor could cause a tragic sermon!* Planned humor can help prevent this from occurring. You do not play recklessly with something so closely related to tragedy. To play carelessly with humor would be like closing your eyes to the kind of snake you have in your hands. It could be rubber; it could be real! It *could* be funny; it *could* be tragic. Planned humor takes into consideration all the factors discussed in Part I of this book. Is the thrust of the humor far enough removed from the pain that exists in the audience? Remember, a preacher would not tell a story about a drunk at an AA meeting—unless that preacher were an alcoholic himself! If

he were one of them, he would be sharing in their incongruities. And he would then be laughing at himself. If not, he would come off as an outsider who would be laughing *at* his audience. That would throw the audience into a defensive, maybe even hostile, frame of mind. Their incongruities would close in their minds. And they would feel the tragic implication of their involvement with alcohol.

2. *Keep your humor positive.* Does your humor build up or put down? Remember, the only one you can safely put down in a sermon is yourself. And you must not do that if you do not stand in high favor with your audience; if your congregation is tired of you; if they come to church only out of habit; if they merely tolerate you. If you are in low favor with your congregation, and you put yourself down, you will in their minds be agreeing with their negative assessment of you. In their minds you will be closing the gap of any hoped-for incongruity that you had imagined. In that situation you might use a put-down on yourself and get not laughs, but hearty "Amens" from your audience!

If you should ever use the following story, a cursory glance may tell you the joke is on you. It is not. It is on your congregation. And they may not be ready for it. Mine was not. Here is the story: "There was this bootlegger who said to his friends, 'I used to be a preacher before I started bootlegging.'

"They said, 'Why on earth would you change from preaching to bootlegging?'

" 'Two reasons,' he said. 'In the second place you *make* more money. And in the first place you *meet* a better class of people.' "

I thought the story was hilarious. The congregation did not come close to laughing. This turned out to be a put-down of them. So I put the story away. (But I still wonder how many bootleggers, or kinfolks to bootleggers, were in that congregation!)

In your creation of humor your comments must not be congruent with the way things are. If a man is handsome beyond words, talk about his need for a face lift. If a lady is ugly, you do not tell a story that indicates she is ugly. There is a story that has been told over and over by traveling preachers. It goes like this: "People ask me why I take my wife with me. I tell them that she is so ugly that I'd rather take her with me than kiss her goodby." One preacher heard the story and liked it so much that he decided to try it himself. He did, and some of the audience were offended because his wife *was* so ugly that any preacher would rather take her than kiss her goodby!

Pick something positive about the personalities you plan to talk about. And talk about them as if they are not that way. To illustrate: If Barbara is organized to the hilt, you say, "What Barbara needs is better organization." Or if she talks too much, you can comment on how quiet she is. Or if he walks too slow, talk about how fast he travels. Or if he is paunchy, you talk about his exercise program. Or if she is eighty years old, you comment on how fine she looks for a sixty-five-year-old. Or if you are short, talk about how things will be when you grow up. Or if you are abnormally tall, talk about how much you enjoy walking by the statue of the historical figure in the local city park and looking *up* to him.

Let it be repeated. Start and end with a positive interpretation of the person talked about. Let the incongruity be an opposite in a direction that permits an affirmation of the person who is the object of the joke.

3. *Mix the ludicrous* (funny-looking) *and the witty* (the surprise).

Most jokes require surprise, so they soon wear out. In the United Presbyterian Church, there is every year a standard story that is told in meetings throughout the

136

Church. Its useful life is about twelve months, but there are many ministers who count on these stories to last for a decade." [84]

4. *Make your humor a means to a higher end.* Humor for the preacher is not an end in itself. If your humor does not serve a purpose other than trying to be funny, forget it. You will be a clown, not a preacher, if you use it.

> The poorest form of pulpit humor is the anecdote. The packaged funny story is the tool of the comedian, and the preacher is not a comedian. Entertainment that is appropriate for a lecture or a banquet talk would seem condescending in a sermon, a concession to a retarded congregation. There are ready-made jokes that are so appropriate that they serve well, but they should not be featured as special items. "It seems there were . . ." or "Which reminds me of . . ." are not introductions that fit well in sermons.
>
> When something amusing is to be related, it should not be brought in as a joke, but as a sermon illustration that happens to be funny. An after-dinner speaker can drop in humor that has only a pretended connection with the purpose of his talk—a preacher cannot. Humor in sermons has to stay within the main channel of the thought.[85]

5. *Keep your audience in mind as you plan your humor.* The preacher who speaks the ridiculous in a *straight* manner may come off great with an audience who does not know better. He comes off ludicrous with an audience that does know better. For instance, you could say to some congregations: "The King James Bible is God's Bible; all other translations are of the Devil!" And "Amens" would rattle the rafters.

You say that in a congregation of Bible students, and the people would laugh you right out of your clerical collar.

The *straight* that we refer to in this book is God's Truth, not our desires. There is a difference. That difference came through as I listened to a radio preacher who for thirty minutes informed his audience: "Other preachers on the radio do not speak the Truth like I do. They will tell you lies. I always tell you the Truth. Jesus said, 'Know the Truth, and the Truth will make you free.' Every sentence I say is the Truth." He talked in these circles until he came within ten minutes of the end of his program. Then he said, "I told you I would tell you the Truth. And I will. Friends, the Truth is I need your money if I stay on the air!"

6. *Your thesis is never to be funny.* It is *straight* from God—a congruent insight of Grace, forgiveness, faith, hope, love, etc.—and delivered that way. The audience never laughs at that Truth. That Truth is the sublime that reveals the ridiculous in human nature. Never laugh at the things of God.

Ministers are church professionals, and they can get so used to handling sacred things that they treat them with familiarity. Some ministerial humor is painful for members of the church. Ministers' feelings about what is holy may be so intense that they release the tension by jokes. A friend said he shocked the church custodian by saying, as he took off his pulpit robe, "Well, check off another one." It is possible for ministers to forget that their jesting about the sacraments, the Bible, church services, prayer, and their own calling may be profanation.

Phillips Brooks was emphatic about this: "There is another creature who ought to share with the clerical prig the contempt of Christian people. He appears in and out of the pulpit. He lays his hands on the most sacred things, and leaves defilement upon all he touches. He is full of Bible jokes. He talks about the Church's sacred symbols in the language of stale jests that have come down from generations of feeble clerical jesters before him.[86]

D. Let us *look for the right places in the sermon to plan for the use of humor.*
1. *In gathering material for a sermon, do not look for something funny.* But take it if it comes across your search. And it will if *you* in your very *being* develop a sense for sighting incongruities. This material may come to you from an observed incident, an involvement of your own (excluding counseling experiences!), a magazine, newspaper, radio, movie, TV, bumper sticker, or the Bible. Since the Bible reveals the Authority with which you ultimately deal with all other experiences, your text comes from that Book. If you are an expository preacher, the problem of primary material solves itself. Once you get all your material together (you know you have enough for one sermon when it looks like you have enough for two), what looked funny at first glance may not be funny anymore. What did not look funny, now may take on a funny vein. Then, after what you've preached humorously lies dormant for a few days, it may once again not seem funny at all. So you take what material is before you, and what strikes you at that particular time for that particular audience as *straight* or funny, plan to use in that sense.

This approach eliminates most of our old sermons. They are funny as we re-read them—funny that we ever got by preaching them the first time! If you can repeat just one thought from an old sermon (some of our old sermons do not even have one sentence worth repeating!), then use it and release the old notes or manuscript to the sermon graveyard.

Of all these sources, the *Bible remains the primary source* for the *straight* and the humorous. Most of us accept that the

Bible can be exegeted *straight*. Not enough of us realize the validity of a humorous exegesis. Some scripture is written in humor:

> Like a gold ring in a swine's snout is a beautiful woman without discretion.[87]
> Trust in a faithless man in trouble is like a bad tooth or a foot that slips.[88]
> Like a madman who throws firebrands, arrows and death, is the man who deceives his neighbor and says, "I am only joking!" [89]
> A continual dripping on a rainy day and a contentious woman are alike; to restrain her is to restrain the wind or to grasp oil in his right hand.[90]
> For the bed is too short to stretch oneself on it, and the covering too narrow to wrap oneself in it.[91]
> A man cuts him down a cedar, or takes a plane or an oak, or lays hold of some other tree of the forest, which the Lord has planted and the rain has nourished for man to use as fuel. He takes part of it and warms himself, he kindles a fire and bakes bread; then he makes a god and worships it, he molds an image and prostrates himself before it. Half of it he burns in the fire, and on its embers he roasts flesh; he eats the roast till he is satisfied; he also warms himself, and says, "Aha! I am warm, I feel the glow." And the rest of it he makes into a god—his idol!—prostrates himself before it, worships it, and prays to it, saying, "Save me, for thou art my God!" [92]

Jesus pictured the ludicrous as he spoke:

> And he said to them, "You have a fine way of rejecting the commandment of God, in order to keep your tradition!" [93]

"Why do you see the speck that is in your brother's eye, but do not notice the log that is in your own eye?" [94]

"You blind guides, straining out a gnat and swallowing a camel!" [95]

"But to what shall I compare this generation? It is like children sitting in the marketplaces and calling to their playmates,

'We piped to you, and you did not dance; we wailed, and you did not mourn.' " [96]

A humorous paraphrase of some Bible stories makes the basic congruent thesis (the truth) come alive. The story of Jonah lends itself to this manner of story-telling.

JONAH

Jonah, God's prophet, lived in Palestine and prophesied with great courage against the faraway Assyrians. When these foreigners stormed at his people overland, Jonah went underground. As they rode away with their bounty from a burned-out Palestine, Jonah fumed. He ran after them, shook his fist at the backs of their heads and said, "You stinkers, God is going to destroy you!"

God said to Jonah, "The Ninevites' wickedness stinks to high heaven."

Jonah said, "You're telling me!"

God said, "I am going to destroy Nineveh."

Jonah said, "Go get 'um! They deserve it!"

"I'm sending you to tell them for me, Jonah," said God.

"You're what?" said Jonah.

God said, "I'm sending you to tell them."

"I wish you had not said that," said Jonah.

Jonah said to himself, "I am not going to Nineveh."

While God was not looking, Jonah slipped down to the sea at Joppa, stood in line for his ticket, sneaking a glance every now and then to see if God were watching, and climbed on board a ship headed for Tarshish, a direction opposite to Nineveh. He made sure God would not find him when he holed up in the hold of the ship. The ship sailed off peacefully. "God cannot find me now," he said to himself as he fell asleep snuggled among the baggage.

Suddenly from out of nowhere came a violent wind upon the sea. The tempest raged. Sails ripped. The mast snapped. Cargo shifted. Jonah bounced. But he never uttered a sound. God blew in looking for Jonah. And Jonah knew it. The scared sailors rowed and rowed and things got worse. They began to pray. They prayed to every god they knew, and looked for more. The captain opened up the hold and hollered, "Is there a Jonah down there?"

Jonah said, "Uh huh."

"Man, this is no time to sleep. Get up and pray to your god. Perhaps he will spare us a thought and save us," he said.

The prophet thought, "I can't do that. If I pray to Yahweh, He'll know where to find me."

Jonah felt relieved when they said, "Let's draw straws in order to find out who is responsible for this evil put upon us." He felt awful when he came up with the short end of the stick. He knew all along that he was the culprit, and now they knew it.

One sailor said to Jonah: "What is your business?"

Others asked, "Where do you come from?"–"What is your country?"–"What is your nationality?"

He replied, "I am a Hebrew, and I worship Yahweh, the God of heaven, who made the sea and the land."

They said, "And you do not pray? What a strange way to worship!"

"What on earth and sea have you done?" they asked. (They should have asked, "What have you *not* done?")

"I am running from Him," he said.

"Oh, no!" they cried, "A servant running from his master.

142

What are we going to do with you? There is only one thing left to do."

They looked up into the heavens where Jonah told them God lived, pointed to Jonah, and said to Yahweh, "Here he is!—over here!" After they got God's attention the sailors said to the prophet's God: "This is not our battle. This is between you and this runaway servant. If you throw much more of this wind and water at him, *we'll* drown for sure."

Jonah held up his hand and said, "May I have your attention?"

They turned to Jonah and said, "If you've got something to say, say it—fast!"

Jonah said, "I have a suggestion—not a good one—you probably would not want to do it—it would be about the most cruel and uncivil thing you could do—but you could throw me overboard."

"Well, have it *your* way," they said.

"Ka plunk!" Over the side he went—head first.

The storm settled. The sailors and the seas calmed, but not Jonah. He bobbled like a drifting cork. So hungry he could eat a raw fish. A raw fish came along and gulped him down. From inside the fish Jonah looked around, surveyed his situation as to what to do next, and concluded: "I think it is time to pray." For three days Jonah prayed. He talked to God like never before. He prayed his prayer; edited it; refined it; re-prayed it. And concluded the polished prayer with: "But I, with a song of praise, will sacrifice to you. The vow I have made, I will fulfill. Salvation comes from Yahweh."

God spoke to the fish and said, "How do you feel?"

The fish, sick at his stomach with Jonah's hypocrisy, up-chucked. Out came Jonah. He hit the ground running. He ran, and he ran, and he ran. Finally out of breath he stood—wet, pale, puckered, shaky, and submissive.

"Where are you going *now,* Jonah?" God asked.

"Nineveh," Jonah answered.

Jonah arrived at Nineveh, a city so sprawling that it took him three days to cross it. God gave Jonah the sermon to preach. Here it is in its entirety: "Only forty days more and Nineveh will be destroyed." Jonah gladly preached to the Ninevite Gentiles. He put a lot of punch into the one-liner. He did not have many words. But how he said them made the sermon a masterpiece on the horrors of God's judgment. He felt they deserved the punishment, and described it with that conviction. He told them they were going to hell, and smiled when he said it.

Then something happened he had not planned on—the people repented. His harsh message of judgment came off *too* convincingly. Even the king of Nineveh put on sack-cloth, sat in ashes, ate no food, drank no water, and commanded all men and beasts to do the same. Men, camels, sheep, goats—everybody and everything repented. The king believed in Yahweh and made believers out of others.

"Who knows?" questioned the king. "Maybe God's burning wrath that this *good* prophet has told us about will turn to love and mercy." And that happened—God changed his mind and spared the people. They could never thank Jonah enough for his delightful sermon on the harshness of God's judgment.

Jonah turned on God in raging frustration: "See, I told you. I told you. I knew it. I knew it. That's why I went to Tarshish. I figured you'd do something like this."

"I feel that you feel angry," said God.

"You feel right," said Jonah.

"Do you feel right in being angry?" asked God.

"Do I feel right in being angry?" screamed Jonah. "I feel perfectly right. They deserve punishment. But not salvation."

"I know, and I agree," said God.

"Good Lord, you don't make sense to me," said Jonah.

"You're right," said God. "But I make sense to Me."

"Well, go ahead and save them, but kill me. I might as well be dead," said Jonah.

"Are you sure you are right to be angry?" God asked.

Jonah answered in a stomp out to a hill on the east side of the city. "Maybe, just maybe," he thought, "God will see His mistake, and wipe them out anyway." He made himself a crude shelter, and sat in the shade of it. God sent a gourd vine to cover the shelter. It cooled things off. This shade delighted Jonah. "Ahhh, now God's seeing things my way," Jonah thought. In comfort he sat back and waited for calamity to strike. And strike it did. At dawn the next day God sent a worm to attack the plant. The worm struck the final blow to the plant and to Jonah. The scorching east wind blew dust in Jonah's face. The sun beat down hard on his head. The heat was on Jonah. Jonah began again to say: "I might as well be dead."

God said to Jonah, "You seem a bit upset. Are you right to be angry about the dead gourd plant?"

Jonah replied, "I have every right to be angry. You used bad judgment when you saved Nineveh. And when you took away my shade, that was the last straw. Yessir. I am angry; angry enough to die."

God said, "You are upset about the loss of a plant that cost you nothing, that you did not make grow, that sprouted and perished in a night, that brought comfort to you—why shouldn't I be concerned for this city of people who belong to me?"

The incongruities in Esther lend themselves easily to a humorous paraphrase.

ESTHER

In the days of Persia's King Ahasuerus the Jews lived as slaves. The privileged Jews were servants. They served the banquet held to display the riches and splendor of the king's empire and the pomp and glory of his majesty. Before all the princes, servants, army chiefs, nobles, and governors of the provinces the King showed his stuff. The festivities went on for 180 days. That party finally pooped. But not the King. He put on another party for those living in the citadel of Susa. In the enclosure adjoining the palace, the king pomped and gloried amongst the white and violet hangings fastened with cords of fine linen and purple thread to silver rings on marble columns, couches of gold and silver on a pavement of porphyry, marble, mother-of-pearl, and precious stones. The servant-Jews told their fellow slaves what they saw. The people's eyes goggled at what they heard.

The party-goers drank their royal wine from royal golden cups of royal ornate design. And they fell in a drunken stupor like twisted pieces of modern sculpture on the royal marble floor. Non-drinkers drank in the royal beauty, and swooned at the sight.

While King Ahasuerus was out with the boys, Queen Vashti decided to have her own party for the women in the royal palace. On the seventh day, when the King was merry with wine (by that time he would be merry!), he ordered seven eunuchs in his attendance to bring before him Queen Vashti, crowned with her royal diadem, in order to display her beauty. He felt her beauty would make him look better to the people. The people felt the King needed all the help he could get with his looks.

Queen Vashti said to the king-wino, "Why, no, I will not go to your party."

The king fussed and fumed, ranted and raged at the absent queen, "She has ruined my party!" While he had been merry, he now was quite contrary.

Wise men, versed in writing and interpreting laws for others to keep, said to the king, "We want to make you happy. You don't deserve to be treated like a dog."

The king said, "You're doggone right, I don't."

The wise men said, "If you let her get by with this, you will have all our wives disobeying us, and you will be getting long distance calls night and day from husbands whose wives have abused them. People would laugh at you as the most wife-abused king in all of history."

King Ahasuerus said, "That must not happen. My history has always been my favorite subject."

"And besides," the wise men continued, "it is for our wives' own good that you do not let the Queen get by with her show of independence. They would assume they have rights. And it would ruin their place in society. And you, O King, would not want to be the cause of their ruin."

"Of course not," said the king. He continued, "I am the king. My orders must be obeyed. I order you: tell me what to do."

The wise men answered, "If it is the king's pleasure, let him issue a royal edict to be irrevocably incorporated into the laws of the Persians and Medes, to the effect that Vashti is never to appear again before King Ahasuerus, and let the king confer the royal dignity on a worthier woman, a woman who walks tall, small talks, and possesses a superior humility."

"Will she make me look good?" he asked.

"With her at your side you will attract people far and wide," they said.

"I feel the pleasure already," he said. "Send the edict. Vashti's punishment will keep the wives in their place, and bring one to my place." He sent letters to all the provinces of the kingdom. They told how Vashti had been banned from the King's presence. The letter did not tell how pleased Vashti was with this "punishment."

The counselors to the king brought home these letters from the king and said to their wives, "Look what the king says."

The wives read the edict, and snickered under their breath

at the lonely condition in which the banishment of Vashti left the king.

The husbands said to their wives, "Isn't it a fine thing that the King has done with Queen Vashti? Doesn't it make you feel secure?"

The wise wives said, "Every time we think about the King, we think of how fine it is."

The King began to regret his harsh treatment of Vashti. He missed her. Her punishment was about to kill him. Before he could regret it very much, the wise men accelerated the program of finding a new Queen. They suggested he take up the hobby of girl-watching. They had often noticed he had talents in that direction. They said, "Let beautiful girls be selected for the king. Let the king appoint commissioners throughout the provinces of his realm to bring all the beautiful young virgins to the citadel of Susa, to the harem under the authority of Hegai the king's eunuch, custodian of the women. Let him provide them with what they need for their adornment, and let the girl who pleases the king take Vashti's place as queen." This new challenge convinced the king he had not dealt too harshly with Vashti. He took this advice—to the people.

Now in the Citadel of Susa there lived a Jew called Mordecai—of the tribe of Benjamin, who had been deported from Jerusalem among captives taken away with King Jeconiah, king of Judah, by Nebuchadnezzar, king of Babylon. He had brought up Hadassah (meaning "myrtle" in Hebrew), his uncle's daughter, who had lost both father and mother. On the death of her parents, Mordecai adopted Cousin Myrtle as his niece. The girl had a good figure and a beautiful face. Mordecai was proud to be her uncle.

Following the mailout of the king's edict, servants brought a great number of girls to the citadel of Susa and entrusted them to Hegai. Among the group was Myrtle. The girl pleased Hegai and won his favor. He quickly provided her with all she needed for her dressing room. Gourmet foods graced her table. He gave her seven special maids from the king's household and transferred her and her maids to the best part of the harem.

Mordecai had forbidden Myrtle to reveal her race or kindred. He felt uncomfortable about Myrtle being in the harem. Mordecai walked up and down in front of the courtyard of the harem every day to make sure Myrtle was not being treated in a harem-skarem manner. Words could not express how well Hegai treated Myrtle. That bothered Mordecai!

Thanks to Hegai's excellent vision, he saw in Myrtle what meets the eye, and more too. He saw and planned a future for her in the king's palace.

All the girls prepared for their appearance before the king. They primped, combed, painted, brushed, clipped, and filed. They filled in the low places and smoothed out the rough ones. They exercised and lost pounds. The masseuses pounded their flesh into better distributed positions. Their competition for "Cinderella's glass slipper" sometimes turned into shouting matches that brought into play a shove here and a push there. They looked their best as Hegai ran them before the king like cows in a hurried auction. Inside they went. One spin around and out the chute. And then Myrtle glided into the arena. Before the king her grace swept away the masked images of all others like a fresh wind that blows away pests. Her immaculate beauty spun him around. And they went out the chute together!

After he got himself under control, the king placed the royal diadem on her head, and proclaimed her Queen instead of Vashti. The king changed the Hebrew "Myrtle" to the Babylonian "Esther." Then the king honored Esther with a banquet. He put her up for all his administrators and ministers to see and admire. He decreed a holiday for all the provinces, and distributed gifts with royal lavishness. At Esther's banquet a case of the struts came on the king. Every time he looked at Esther he strutted. Esther's presence changed the countenance of the king. The people could look at the king and tell she was beautiful.

While Esther was now queen, she remained loyal to Mordecai. At this time Mordecai worked in the office of the chancellor. Two malcontents, Bigthan and Teresh, king's eunuchs who were guardians of the chancellery entrance, plotted to assassinate King Ahasuerus. Mordecai heard about this and informed Queen Esther, who in turn, on Mordecai's authority, told the king. An investigation of the matter proved the report to be true. The gallows claimed the two conspirators, and the incident was recorded in the Book of Chronicles in the presence of the king. Mordecai made points with the king, and the chroniclers recorded the score.

Shortly afterwards, King Ahasuerus singled out Haman, from the land of Agag, for promotion. Since Agag is the name of an Amalekite king conquered by Saul the Benjaminite (I Samuel 15:7-9), there was no love lost between Mordecai the Benjaminite and Haman the Agagite. The king gave Haman authority, second only to himself. The king ordered all the people to bow down before Haman. Everybody did, except Mordecai. Saul did not bow before Agag in his day; Mordecai would not bow before Haman. "Why do you flout the royal command?" the officials of the Chancellery asked Mordecai. They asked him this day after day, but he took no notice of them. In the end they reported the matter to Haman. They wanted to see whether Mordecai would persist in his attitude, since he had told them he was a Jew. Haman decided to see for himself whether Mordecai would bow down or not. Haman made it a point to walk close enough for Mordecai to bow. He walked as close to Mordecai as he could without bumping him. Mordecai never noticed Haman. Haman stood there until finally Mordecai looked at Haman. And he looked. And he looked. But he never bowed. Haman nearly had a seizure. He stomped off in a huff when Mordecai would not bow down.

Now he planned Mordecai's murder. His fury grew, and he planned the murder of Mordecai's family. He finally made up his mind to wipe out all the members of Mordecai's race, the Jews, throughout the empire of Ahasuerus.

Haman had decided his course of action. He cast lots to determine the best day to release his fury on the Jews. After picking his day, Haman said to King Ahasuerus, "There is a certain unassimilated nation scattered among the other nations throughout the provinces of your realm; their laws are different from those of all the other nations and they ignore the royal edicts; hence it is not in the king's interest to tolerate them. If it pleases the king to decree their destruction, I am prepared to pay 10,000 talents of silver to the king's receivers, to be credited to the royal treasury." That amounted to $18,000,000, two-thirds of the annual revenue of the Persian empire. He felt the exaggerated figure would lift up the importance of the matter in the king's mind. And it also made Haman sound sacrificial—even though he could have never paid off.

The king, with his mind on other things, hardly heard Haman. He simply said to Haman: "Keep the money and you can have the people too; do what you like with them."

Runners took the murder message far and wide to the people of all the provinces.

When Mordecai learned what happened, he tore his garments and put on sackcloth and ashes. Then he went through the city, wailing loud and bitterly, until he arrived in front of the Chancellery. He was not allowed to enter because he wore sackcloth. All across the province the people mourned and fasted. They wept and they wailed, and many lay on sackcloth and ashes. This made Haman very happy.

When Queen Esther's maids and eunuchs came and told her about Mordecai's mourning, she was overcome with grief. She sent clothes for Mordecai to put on instead of his sackcloth, but he would not wear them. Esther knew that Mordecai had a reason for his peculiar action. The reason came to her through an eunuch. Mordecai wanted her to go to the king and plead her people's case. She sent back this message: "If I approach the king without being summoned, I am a dead Jewess. Only a raised scepter in the hand of the king can save me." Mordecai came back with: "You are a dead Jewess if you don't. Who knows? Perhaps you have come to the throne for just such a time as this."

That did it. Esther sent this reply: "Get all the Jews of Susa together and fast for three days. I and my maids will do the same. After that I shall go to the king in spite of the law; and if I perish, I perish." Quickly they fasted and she did too. On the third morning, she took off her mourning attire and dressed herself in full splendor. She took off, put on, washed and dried, smeared, wiped, powdered, clipped, combed, and brushed until she was prepared for the beauty contest she could not afford to lose. The crucial moment had arrived. The time came to go into the king's presence. With a delicate air she leaned on one maid, while another maid carried her train. They lifted her robes that swept the ground. She looked her best, but felt her worst. She passed through door after door. Then she stepped into the presence of the king—a formidable sight to the queen. Her heart shrank with fear. There he was in all his power, glory, pomp and majesty—that turned to putty at the sight of Esther! Like a flash, the golden scepter went up. And so did her stock. He spared himself the loss of her presence.

She pleased him. He saw in her everything he wanted.

He then became everything she wanted when he caught her distress signal.

"What is the matter, Queen Esther? Tell me what you desire; even if it is half of my kingdom, I grant it to you," the king said.

"Would the king be pleased," Esther replied, "to come today to the banquet I have prepared for Haman?"

The king said, "Tell Haman to come at once, so that Esther may have her wish."

So the king and Haman came to the banquet that Esther had prepared. Haman felt like he was on top of the world. He drank it all in as they drank their wine. The king again said to Esther, "Tell me what you request; I grant it to you. Tell me what you desire; even if it is half my kingdom, it is yours for the asking."

"What do I desire, what do I request?" Esther replied. "If I have found favor in the king's eyes, and if it is his pleasure to grant what I ask and to agree to my request, let the king and Haman come to the other banquet I intend to give tomorrow, and then I will do as the king says." (She will do as the king says when she feels he will say what she wants.)

Haman left full of joy and high spirits that day (he did not know Esther was a Jewess). But, when Mordecai ignored him again at the Chancellery, a gust of anger displaced his joy. He held himself back from saying anything, however, and went home. Haman sent for his friends and Zeresh his wife. He boasted to them about his dazzling wealth, his many children, how the king had raised him to a position of honor and promoted him over the heads of the king's administrators and ministers. "What is more," he added, "Queen Esther just invited me and the king—no one else except me and the king—to a banquet she was giving, and better still, she has invited me and the king again tomorrow."

His swelled head began to heat up as he continued, "But what do I care about all this when all the while I see Mordecai the Jew hanging around the Chancellery? He won't bow. He won't even speak to me!"

"Have him hanging around outside your window at home. Have an eighty-three-foot gallows run up," Zeresh his wife and all his friends said, "and in the morning ask the king to have Mordecai hanged on it. Then accompany the king to the feast without a care in the world!" Delighted with this advice, Haman had the gallows erected. A gallows eighty-three feet high! Haman prepared for the hanging of the century.

That night, the king could not sleep. He liked bedtime stories read from the Record Book. He asked that the Chronicles be brought and read to him. The king got drowsy and almost nodded off to sleep as he listened to the account of how two men had planned to murder "the king."

"The king! that's me!" cried the king as he jumped to his feet wide awake. "Who tried to kill me?" he asked.

The reader said, "Bigthan and Teresh, eunuchs who were guardians of the Threshold."

"Who was the informant?" the king asked.

"Mordecai," they answered.

"And what honor and dignity," the king asked, "was conferred on Mordecai for this?"

"Nothing has been done for him," the courtiers in attendance replied.

(Haman had at the precise moment entered the outer ante-chamber of the king's palace to ask the king to have Mordecai hanged on the gallows that he had just put up for the purpose.)

The king's courtiers replied, "Haman is waiting in the ante-chamber."

"Bring him in," the king said. Haman entered. Before Haman could say a word about his gallows for Mordecai the king said, "What is the right way to treat a man whom the king wishes to honor?"

"Oh boy," thought Haman, "more honors for me! Whom would the king wish to honor, if not me?" So he thought up the highest honors he could conceive and said, "If the king wishes to honor someone, have royal robes brought which the king has worn, and a horse which the king has ridden, with a royal diadem on its head. The robes and the horse should be handed to one of the noblest of the king's officers, and he should array the man whom the king wishes to honor and lead him on horseback through the city square, proclaiming before him: 'This is the way to treat a man whom the king wishes to honor!' "

"You are the noblest, aren't you?" asked the king.

"Yessir," said Haman.

"Hurry," the king said to Haman, "Since you are the noblest of all, you take the horse and do everything you have just said to Mordecai the Jew, who works at the Chancellery. On no account leave anything out that you have mentioned."

Haman's heart sank into his stomach. His mouth filled with cotton. His blood drained from his face. He nearly died there on the spot.

The king said, "What's the matter? Don't you like my idea?"

Haman said in a forced, squeaky voice, "I would have never thought of such an idea in all my life."

Haman did as the king ordered. He took royal robes and put them on Mordecai. Then he lifted Mordecai onto the king's horse, and led him on horseback to the city square. Around and around the city square he led the horse with Mordecai riding, and constantly called out: "This is the way to treat a man whom the king wishes to honor!"

This was Mordecai's finest hour; the worst for Haman.

After his royal ride through the city square, Mordecai returned to the Chancellery. Haman hurried home so embarrassed that he covered his face so nobody could see him. He told his wife Zeresh and all his friends what had happened. They said, "It's been nice knowing you. Thanks to Mordecai you have had it! Since he belongs to the Jewish race, you will never recover the upper hand again. Thanks to him, you will fall and fall again." As they talked Haman sank, and sank, and sank.

While they were still talking, the king's eunuchs arrived and in a hurry escorted a sagging Haman to the banquet that Esther had prepared. At the party Haman had little to say. At every utterance of the king Haman would say, "I'll drink to that." As he gulped down his wine, he heard the king again say to Esther, "Tell me what you request, Queen Esther. I grant it to you. Tell me your desire; even if it is half my kingdom, it is yours for the asking."

"I'll drink to that," said Haman as he tried to bury his problems.

"If I have found favor in your eyes, O King," Queen Esther replied, "and if it pleases your majesty, grant me my life—that is what I request; and the lives of my people—that is what I desire. For we are doomed, I and my people, to destruction, slaughter and annihilation. If we had merely been condemned to become slaves and servant-girls, I would have said nothing. Furthermore, it will be beyond the means of *the persecutor* to pay the 10,000 talents he has promised the king in return for the death of my people. He is a liar as well as a murderer!"

King Ahasuerus interrupted Queen Esther, "Who is this man?" He asked, "Where is he, the schemer of such an outrage?"

Esther replied, "The persecutor, the enemy? Why, this wretched Haman!"

The party spirit left Haman. He could not drink to that! He could hardly swallow! He felt now his problems would be buried with him! Haman quaked in the presence of the king and queen. In a rage the king rose and left the banquet to go into the palace garden to get a breath of fresh air and a clear head. Haman realized that the king was having some last thoughts about him. He stayed behind and begged Queen Esther for his life. He climbed upon her couch and pleaded for her to realize that this was merely a communication problem. "I meant no harm. I was just teasing," he said.

When the king returned from the palace garden into the banquet hall, he found Haman huddled across the couch where Esther was reclining. "What!" the king exclaimed. "Is he going to rape the queen before my eyes in my own palace?"

The words were scarcely out of his mouth when a eunuch threw a veil over Haman's face. That meant death for Haman. Harbona, one of the eunuchs attending the king, said, "How convenient! There is that eighty-three-foot gallows that Haman built to hang Mordecai on. Remember, Mordecai saved the king's life. The gallows stands at Haman's house."

"Hang him on it!" said the king. So Haman hung around at the end of his rope on the gallows that he had erected for Mordecai.

A benevolent spirit surfaced as the king's wrath subsided. A letter written in the name of the king revoked the "irrevocable decree" sent out by Haman earlier. The king granted permission to the Jews across the kingdom to take care of their enemies any way they saw fit.

That same day King Ahasuerus gave Queen Esther the house of Haman, the persecutor of the Jews. Esther revealed to the king that Mordecai was her cousin. The king, who had taken back his signet ring from Haman, now gave it to Mordecai. And Esther gave Mordecai charge of Haman's house. Mordecai traded his sackcloth for a princely gown of violet and white, with a great golden crown and a cloak of fine linen and purple. The city of Susa shouted and cheered when they saw him. Mordecai enjoyed waving at the admiring crowds as he rode away on his "high horse." [98]

2. *Since humor catches attention, it may be used in the introduction.* Whether you use a one-point, two-point, or three-point sermon (any more points than this and you probably have that many more sermons in the sermon!), you will have

157

an introduction. You will have it whether you plan it or not. It may be a "harumphh!," or a scratching of the head, or a particular sign that something is about to come forth. Since you are going to have an introduction of some sort anyway, it is futile to argue whether you should or should not, will or will not. A better beginning may be had if you plan it. On the other hand, a better beginning may be had if you do not plan it. If that is the case, then plan not to plan it. Plan for it to come off "spontaneously." You know what this does to a manuscript reader. You do not "spontaneously" read a manuscript. However, a planned comment in the manuscript that allows you to look at your audience may come off "spontaneously."

Since whatever you do as an introduction gets attention, you may plan some time to use humor. This should not be planned for every sermon because the audience will come to expect you to be funny. That expectation does away with the surprise element that makes up much of your humor. The consistently opening funny statement is the work of the comic. His audience comes geared for humor. They expect him to start, continue, and end with humor. The preacher plans for his humor to complement his essentially *straight* performance. He can use humor in his introduction—sparingly.

In telling Bible stories, you may picture them in a ludicrous manner. But they will begin after you have made a *straight* opening statement. In this case, the ludicrous Bible story gains audience attention *for* the *straight* introductory statement that in all likelihood would be your thesis sentence.

If you tell a fairly long Bible story in humor, that is enough humor for that sermon. If you choose a pericope of scriptures to explain your thesis (if you do not have a thesis, get one, and send your audience home with at least one good thought), or if you choose a topic to discuss, you may plan to use humor in the introduction.

The late Dr. Halford Luccock, a prominent professor of homiletics, sometimes used humor to begin his sermons. In his opening statement in the sermon *After Church Was Over* he writes:

> *Now when the synagogue broke up, many of the Jews and devout proselytes followed Paul and Barnabas; who, speaking to them, urged them to continue in the grace of God.* —Acts 13:43
>
> This conclusion to the Sabbath service does not follow the pattern so familiar to us. We know all too well the dismal anti-climax which often follows when "the synagogue breaks up." The congregation goes home to dinner, or there is a kindly, "That was a fine sermon, doctor," which forms a cheery requiem over an already buried truth. Perhaps, later on, the service comes to mind fleetingly in a lament that the soprano flats her high notes so often.[99]

3. *The body of the sermon may be strengthened with a limited use of humor.* It relaxes the strain of listening, grabs back the audience's wandering mind, and puts over the point illustrated. The late Dr. R. G. Lee preached *straight* sermons with a light sprinkling of humor. But those humorous instances brought home his point so well that his hearers would more easily remember the subject. In his sermon *Redeeming the Time* Dr. Lee used humor few times. But what he used was adequate. Here is one of these instances. He quoted an Atlanta editor: "Some people stay longer in an hour than others do in a week." Then Dr. Lee continued, "I suppose President Coolidge found that out when the old countryman visited him, and he looked like he didn't know when to leave. And he stayed more than some of his Cabinet would have stayed in two or three days. When the old farmer went home, they asked him if he got to talk with the Presi-

dent. And he said, 'Yes, and you know, he's the politest man I ever saw. He got up and shook hands with me three times before I left!' " [100]

Dr. Lee vividly illustrated his thesis in his sermon *The Contemporary* with this ludicrous story:

> Once, by invitation of a friend, I attended a big football game. They told me that seventy thousand folks were there. I did not count them. But if I am ever as sure of having $70,000 as I am that the seventy thousand people were there, then a fortune is mine—sometime. Moreover, all, young and old, were eager, expectant, excited.
>
> On both sides of the huge bowl were four blaring brass bands, with every fife screaming, with every trumpet in full blast, with every cornet sounding loudly forth, with every saxophone gutturally whining, with every big horn bellowing forth a bass, with every drum moaning its unmuffled noise, with every flute cajolingly uttering its voice. The cheer leaders from both universities were cutting capers in front of the student sections and calling their hosts of "rooters" to loud cheers through raucous megaphones, while the cheer hosts responded in full lung. What with the flying ribbons and colors, what with the bands all aflare, what with rumble of voices in conversation, a jovial hysterical tempest seemed to be raging in that huge bowl!
>
> When the game started and the seventy thousand folks who witnessed the spectacle, waving flaming colors and pennants, singing madly, shouting excitedly, screaming wildly, roaring in elation or disappointment, as the battle waged, now in favor of one team, now of the other, I recalled a tornado I had once seen and heard. I could imagine myself seeing a volcano in eruption, throwing forth gaudy blossoms in profusion as

160

I watched that madly shouting crowd throw hats and pennants in the air, waving ribbons all the while. An earthquake seemed to be rumbling and growling throughout that vast arena.

And, all during the game, the football, which the forty-four eyes of the alert players in the stadium followed and upon which 140,000 eyes from the grandstands were fixed, went back and forth, to and fro, hither and yon—sometimes kicked by skilled toe, sometimes carried by strong arms behind trained interference, sometimes thrown the forward pass route by muscular arm. And, till the very last minute of play, that vast throng, the strong voices of youth, and the quivering voices of old age mingling in one riotous clamor, seemed never to weary with their cheers.

And I, from my seat high up on the last row, watched the eleven fellows, now the eleven fellows on one team, now the eleven fellows on the other team, carrying that ball toward the goal.

To what were they listening?

To the clamorous urge of the brass bands? No.

To the wild surge of cheering host? No.

To the roar of thousands of voices? No.

To the call of cheer leaders? No.

I noticed the little lithe quarterback on each team, as the ball was in his possession, as he called his signals, as the throngs watched to see what play was coming.

"Twenty-nine, forty-two, eighty-three, hike" that quarterback would call. Or, "Sixteen, twenty-two, thirty-three, on!" And, as the ball was put into play, we all got evidence, thrilling evidence, that these eleven husky men were giving ear to and obedience to one voice—*to just one voice.* Yes, to the voice of the quarterback, given authority to run that team, their ears were keenly sensitized.[101]

161

In his sermon *Great Is the Lord,* Dr. Lee put together a gem:

> I had in mind how far short many Christians fall in meeting their ambassadorial assignments when I preached to my people once on "Bantam Baptists." I could talk (with tears, too) about midget Methodists, pewter Presbyterians, lilliputian Lutherans, puny Pentacostals, miniature Mennonites, diminutive Disciples, and effervescing Episcopalians—because there are many mediocrities among members of all our churches.[102]

Dr. Lee's light touch characterized much of his humor. In his sermon *The Saving Name of Jesus,* he exercises his lightest touch of humor:

> Not a name that entangles men's tongues or presents perplexities or hesitancy in pronunciation. Though Jesus is the overtopping character of all time, his name is not difficult of pronunciation—like Artaxerxes, Belteshenesh, Chermonesus, Nebuchadnezzar.[103]

In his long list of city characterizations in his sermon *The Perfect City,* he writes:

> New Orleans—most interesting city in the world.
> Chicago—noted for schools and underworld characters.
> San Francisco—remembered for its earthquake and fire.
> Los Angeles—with more "isms" that ought to become "wasms" than any city in America.
> ------
> Istanbul—noted for dirt and devotion to Islamism.[104]

Dr. Halford Luccock also used humor without becoming a comic. Though, to hear him tell it, even his best *straight* sermon ideas came in a funny way. He would be driving along the street, and suddenly the car would get over the middle line, or run off the shoulder of the road, or plow through a red light. His wife would then call him back to the task of driving the auto. She and he knew what was happening. He was "having a sermon." He would tell his hearers that sermons always had a way of translating themselves in his driving.

Dr. Luccock chose his topic and used an appropriate amount of humor to get his point across. In his sermon *Externalism*, he illustrated his point with this story:

There is a striking disproportion between the greatness of man's inventions and the triviality of the uses to which they are frequently put. This is particularly true of the latest wonder which science has put into man's hands—the radio. Sometimes we get a glimpse of the possible service of the radio to life's highest values, as in the broadcast of the opening session of the London Conference on Disarmament, or of great music. But more frequently there is a stronger impression of the contrast between the wonder of the process and the insanity of the message going over the air. Thoreau made a similar observation many years ago when the first Atlantic cable was laid. To someone exclaiming over the marvel of it, Thoreau said, "Yes, it is wonderful. Probably the first news that comes over it will be that Princess Adelaide has the whooping cough." Anyone who has listened to dreary hours of advertising ballyhoo over the radio will feel the force of Thoreau's statement that "we have improved means of unimproved ends." Speaking of this aspect of the radio, Mr. Chesterton observed that "it is rather remarkable that the most amazing means of communication should have been developed at the precise moment in history when nobody had anything to say." [105]

In his sermon *What Do You Select From Experience?* he made sure his audience remembered his thesis when he said:

> There is a vast difference between those who contend for a newly discovered truth or a new stirring of Christian conscience which impels action in a "dangerous" field, and those who accept the results of these pioneer endeavors after they have been established. It is easy enough to "get on the band wagon."
>
> A football referee was once asked concerning a certain player in a game which he had refereed. "I can only say this," he answered, "I have never had to pull him out from the bottom of a scrimmage. I have often found him on the top of a pile of players, where he had jumped on after the man with the ball had been stopped by another player. He was never the first to make the tackle." There are a good many players of that sort. It is a safe game to play. One is not nearly as likely to get hurt if he waits until the ball is "down." So we have many who valiantly come out for positions which have become quite safe and popular, or denounce evils which have no longer any powerful friends.[106]

4. Through these usages, humor gets attention and makes for retention. This works satisfactorily in the introduction and the body of the sermon. But *humor by its nature is not used in a sermon conclusion.* Humor is an incongruity, a disparity, an inconsistency, a knee-jerk reaction to a gap between what is and what ought to be, between how we act and

what we are. You cannot end on a high note of optimism, a plea, a promise, a warning, or a quiet note that commits the decision to the hearers—humorously. You do not end a sermon with the gap that makes for laughter, but with a *straight* comment, with a Truth.

E. If you have never used humor, begin with very little. Get a feel for the purpose of humor, and move forward with the use of humor as your own sense develops.

If you have used humor, *these guidelines and suggestions can help you study your use of humor.* If you blindly trust that you have been given the perfect sense of humor, you are probably making your congregation miserable. Your reading of this material should help them considerably.

PART VI

HUMOR IN THE PULPIT-PREACHING SITUATION

HUMOR IN THE
PULPIT-PREACHING
SITUATION

A. All that we have talked about now comes to *the testing place*. That place is the pulpit-preaching situation, where good humor is needed. The following musing illustrates that humor goes to church precisely because people are there—along with God's Truth that illumines incongruities.

A LAUGH IN CHURCH

When I was a boy, I laughed out in church one day—not at anything the preacher said, but at the fellow in the back of the auditorium who was "with it" in a different sort of way. He went to sleep and used his right shoulder as a pillow. When the preacher said something that was right, we knew it was because the people "Amened" at just that right time. Each time they said "Amen," this man jerked his head upright and echoed the others with his own "Amen."

I very nearly snickered myself to death. I swallowed so much laughter my stomach hurt.

169

After that service my Sunday School teacher lectured me with the words, "Aren't you ashamed laughing like that in church?"

"Yes'm," I answered.

I didn't want to. But she made me lie right then and there.

I felt like saying, "Talk to Mr. Smith. He agreed with the preacher's sermon, and didn't hear a word preached."

But I didn't. Especially I didn't want to disturb the status quo. Many a Sunday Mr. Smith was the best attraction for us kids. He made church-going interesting.

I must confess. I've laughed a thousand times in church. At the soloist who, preceding her singing, asked loudly through the P.A. system, "Am I on?" She always was.

At the man who jumped straight up during the sermon and hollered, "Whooee!" slapped the back of his head and began praying aloud. A wasp had stung him. His reactions from that moment on were more physical than spiritual, though we all agreed that prayer had more feeling in it than any prayer he ever prayed.

At the little boy who in a loud whisper asked his mother, "Mama, what's he (the preacher) saying?" To which she answered, "I don't know. But hush and listen!"

Then there was the time I tried to practice-preach my sermon to an empty sanctuary—gestures and all. I imagined an audience which leaned forward to catch every perfect word and voice inflection—which "Amened" at all the appropriate spots, which were many—which admired me in my new blue suit and dazzling striped blue, yellow, and maroon tie—which flocked to join the church as a result of this great sermon. As I was leaving the sanctuary following this spirited display of the best sermon "they" ever heard I could have sworn I heard Someone laugh. That was the first and last time I practice-preached.

Sweazey calls for the preacher to recognize a place for humor in his sermons.

> It is a mistake for a preacher to subject the congregation to a long face. There are times of great solemnity in a church; there must be sermons that will not make anybody happy. Duty, repentance, and caring about those who suffer must be earnestly presented. But if the prevailing mood of the sermons is somber, it is a denial of the Holy Spirit and a travesty on Christianity. A sour minister is a heretic of the worst sort. "These things have I spoken to you, that my joy may be in you, and that your joy may be full," was Jesus' promise. So the minister does not have to be *too* (my italics) embarrassed if something he says makes people laugh right out in church.[107]

The minister should not be embarrassed *at all* if people laugh right out in church. He should be embarrassed if they cannot laugh at all. No, not "embarrassed." That is a sign of offended pride. He should be repentant. That experience restores him to his true humanity, to a taking of himself less seriously. It restores to him a sense of humor.

The same things can be said for the audience. For with the preacher and the audience, their joy includes humor.

B. *Model for the Pulpit-Preaching Situation.* A good sense of humor lets God inside our churches through the pulpit-preaching situation. The emphasis is on "situation," rather than "preaching," because the over-all situation is itself a part of the "preaching." The following model helps you see more clearly what is being said here.

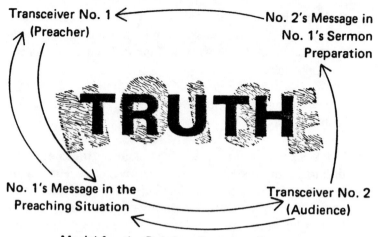

Transceiver No. 1 (Preacher)

No. 2's Message in No. 1's Sermon Preparation

TRUTH

No. 1's Message in the Preaching Situation

Transceiver No. 2 (Audience)

Model for the Pulpit — Preaching Situation

1. *God's Truth tries to break through* every human situation, from the changing of a tire along a hot highway to a worship setting in an air-conditioned building. Sometimes the changing of the tire and finding a flat spare tire teaches us more about preparedness than the best sermon on the subject.

The pulpit-preaching situation is an effort on the part of the preacher and the audience to insure that Truth is heard.

If the preacher and the audience try too hard to make it come off, somebody in that church is going to laugh at their efforts of making sure God is well taken care of—and should! Will Rogers said that humor carried us through the depression. If humor can carry us through a depression, surely it will help your audience get through your sermon!

First, let it be understood that you do not see *the* Truth, but that you see *with* the Truth. The absolute, congruent, straight Truth, "God is Love," comes into every pulpit-preaching through somebody. That is serious. But when somebody gets too close to somebody else's wife or husband,

172

and "mistakes" an extra love affair as "God's Love," that is funny (and tragic too, according to how close you are to that event). Within the same audience, the straight Truth may move some to tears while He (the Holy Spirit) moves others to laugh at incongruities. Some people may laugh; some may cry; some may just blankly sit there. Divine Truth works in all of them.

2. *According to my model of the pulpit-preaching situation Truth works through two transceivers,* the audience and the preacher (the transceiver, a modern communications radio, transmits and receives).

a. *The audience transmits and the preacher receives* while he prepares his sermon. What do they know? What is their background? What are their beliefs? What are their needs? What are their aspirations? The preacher "listens" and with Truth prepares *their* sermon (Part V of this book plugs into the pulpit-preaching situation at this point).

Joe Johnson once had a parishioner who unwittingly (or was it?) spelled out how congregations expect to be heard.

> Years ago I was pastoring so far back in the woods that it required five days for the sunlight to filter through all that chlorophyll.
>
> In one of my primeval churches, perhaps the most faithful attendant was an alcoholic. Back then that dear man was referred to as a "drunk" or a "sot." But he had more sense than most of the other members there, because he never attended when he was sober.
>
> He would sit toward the back, never creating a disturbance although stewed as the proverbial prune. Alas, he was the only person in the congregation with enthusiasm and fire, giving forth with: "Tha's correc', prech'," and "Ar'men." Too bad his fire had to be kindled with fire water.
>
> At the close of the service on a cold, wintry eve, my

inebriated member breathed in my face, and *I* became tipsy. Fraternally plopping his arm around my shoulder, he lushly gushed, "You know some'pin, Preacher, you're the best *pasture* we've ever had!"[108]

Most of your audiences are homogeneous enough for you to evaluate. True, that homogeneity results from man's broken condition. But that remains the only condition the church works under in this world. And humor works well within that setting—where people come together in their educated ignorance and act "Gawdly"—and where God's Truth works anyway by showing you *that is not* the way He is. We recognize that incongruity (scripture calls it hypocrisy) because Truth illumines it for us.

Give your audience credit for having a sense of humor. Learn from them what they see as funny. For the preacher it is not: "I've got a hilarious sense of humor. Hold still and I will give a little of it to you." Quite the contrary. You "hold still" and listen to your audience. You do not tell a joke to an audience as if they were dumb sponges. See with them the incongruities they see. And they will give you credit for having a sense of humor *too!*

The average audience will not accept being told outright that they are wrong in their thinking. They like to think they are consistent in their beliefs and attitudes.

In recent years, several theories of attitude change have been developed. They frequently are referred to as the tension-reduction, or homeostatic theories. Heider's balance theory, Festinger's dissonance theory, and Osgood's congruity theory all have received wide attention. Actually hundreds of experimental studies tend to support one or more of these theories, many of the studies even having been conducted prior to the systematic formulation of the theories.

All these theories have a common basis. This has been called the principle of consistency. These theories suggest that the human mind has a powerful need for consistency in attitudes and beliefs. Thus, if two or more attitudes or beliefs are inconsistent with one another, change in attitude or belief occurs as a result of the mind's effort to establish consistency.[109]

Again Truth reveals that nobody (including the preacher!) is completely consistent because of the incongruities in all of us.

A look with Truth at those inconsistencies through humor allows the audience a glimpse of their gap without alienating them by telling them outright where they are wrong; e.g., say to a male chauvinist audience: "My wife knows who is the head of our house! I'm going to pick up my clothes whether she likes it or not!," or "I'm taking her out to dinner once a week whether she likes it or not!" and you will put them to thinking about their inconsistencies without exploding their consistency patterns.

Love your audience or you will hurt them with your humor. If they have the slightest idea that you do not love them, your comments will not reveal an incongruity, but rather a congruity that kills the effect of humor, e.g., a preacher poked fun at a man he did not like, and he thought it was hilarious humor. The audience went: "Ooooo!" They took his intended humor straight because they knew there was "bad blood" between them. Only those who love with God's Love can exercise good humor. A good rule to remember: never jest with or about someone who does not like you. That person will take it straight, and you will worsen your relationship.

b. When *the preacher* stands in the pulpit-preaching situation, he *transmits and receives*. So does the audience. Whenever an audience "amens," laughs, smiles, or nods affirmatively while you preach, that is their way of saying, "You have just said what I wanted to say." It remains their way of transmitting, of talking, with you. Congregations have been known to have about as much to say as the preacher.

> When his members accuse a black preacher of preaching "white," that's considered an insult. As one black brother observed, "You people keep the Lord locked up and hedged in. Let him loose." Amen![110]

Your good humor helps them in their part of the "conversation." When your good humor makes it easy for them to "talk back" in laughter, your credibility goes up in their minds. You are more believable in what you say. If you do not listen to your audience and do not use humor acceptable to them, your credibility goes down.

Some words our present society and culture will accept; others they will not. For example, "visceral feeling" sounds better than "gut-level"; "when I left the party" sounds better for a preacher to say than "after I left the dance"; and bathroom jokes are out. Bathroom words through the inevitable surprise evoke a shocked laugh. But the after-shocks are not funny. Such was the case with the preacher who told the following story:

> Little Mary (his pre-school daughter) was beside me with some clothes under her arm. She'd had some kind of accident the day before. And I was carrying out five or six pieces of clothing that I was going to take to the dry cleaners. I was going out with the clothes under my arm like this. She was going there beside me with her clothes like this. Going along the walk, we were almost to the car when she looked up at me and said, "Daddy, are you taking those in case you 'TT' too?" I told her, "Yes." I didn't want to disappoint her.

At home among parents and friends that would be accept-
ably funny; in the pulpit, crudely "funny." You just do not
talk about "TTing" in the pulpit, or about anything that de-
rives its "humor" from a surprise comment that is socially
unacceptable in that society and culture.

I fell into the same trap when I told about the "artist" who
displayed her skills in the Impossible Art Show. She hung
her baby's dirty diapers on the line. And she proceeded to
tell the judges how meaning was derived from the various
strains of food stains that spotted the diapers. Asked how she
could justify her display as art, she said, "Because I said so!"
I told that story and nobody smiled. But somebody did
frown. My wife later told me that this story was as bad as
"TTing" in the pulpit. Both stories were too crude for the
pulpit.

Preachers who insist on using these crude sayings in the
pulpit turn to I Samuel 25:22, 24; I Kings 14:10; 16:11;
21:21; II Kings 9:8; 18:27; Isaiah 36:12; and the *Song of
Solomon* (7:1-9) as biblical proofs that their choice of words
is acceptable in the pulpit. I submit for your judgment the
following: the most ardent supporters of biblical preaching
would have a difficult time getting beyond that biblical bathroom jargon to the basic Truth behind the text.

If you lose audience esteem through humor they do not
appreciate, you may still rebuild your credibility through use
of humor acceptable to them. By your continuing use of humor, you show no recognition of audience hostility. That in
itself disarms the audience, and possibly leaves them open to
hear what you have to say. A time of low audience esteem
for the preacher may come following a visit to a worship
service by a pulpit committee from another church, especially when the word gets around that you were not called by
that church! People begin to say, "They come to hear him.
They never call him." In this case you might say: "A pulpit
committee came here last week (assume you are the only one

who knows it). You know how I knew they were a pulpit committee? They sneaked in the doors in pairs. They sat in opposite corners of the auditorium, held the hymn book high in front of their faces, smiled that Guess-what-I-am-doing-here look, brought note books instead of Bibles, and they never said 'Amen.' Silently, they melted into the night without speaking to a soul. If I ever hear from them, I'm going to ask, 'What inner sanctum do you come from?' "

Of course, if they call you, make a big deal over how you turned it down because you already have the best congregation.

It may cause low audience esteem for the preacher if no pulpit committee ever shows. "Doesn't anybody else want our preacher?" some will ask. Here is a way you can handle that. Tell your congregation: "When you have a church as great as I've got, there's just no place left to go." That will baffle any congregation. They cannot afford to disagree with that assessment. And in all likelihood they really feel they are the greatest. With this approach, who knows? You may retire there.

And you have a better chance for a move. People will more likely take a look at you if you do not want to move than if you do. If the word gets out that you do want to move and cannot, then low audience esteem for you will not be a bother. You probably will not even have a congregation!

c. *Seeing what is funny transmits to the audience that you are a man of Truth.* This works as long as you keep your sights on your incongruities, and not on your expert self. If you think you are funny, that self-image will come through your sermon to the audience. And they will think you are silly. Think on the incongruity that you see—on the thing itself that is funny. This perspective permits you to reveal to the audience what Truth has revealed to you (remember, Truth elicits the humor). The next *straight* point you make continues the same Truth-Spirit that revealed the humor.

178

The same Truth produces the *straight* and the humorous. The preacher who stays in touch with that Spirit moves smoothly from the *straight* to the humorous, and vice versa. The attitude of the preacher remains constant as he deals with both the sublime and the ridiculous. He desires, strives, and performs as a man of Truth.

> The preacher must always try to feel what it is like to live inside the skins of the people he is preaching to, to hear the truth as they hear it. That is not as hard as it sounds because, of course, he is himself a hearer of truth as well as a teller of truth, and he listens out of the same emptiness as they do for a truth to fill him and make him true.[111]

Both the preacher and his audience are audiences together under God's incongruity-revealing Truth. Dr. Halford Luccock says concerning humor and religion:

> Religion provides perspective before the greatness of God; humor provides perspective about ourselves and about others. Humor, like religion, has a way of cutting a pompous strutter down to size—humor is a moral banana skin dedicated to the discomfiture of all who take themselves too solemnly.[112]

Only God knows what finally comes out of a pulpit-preaching situation. But if you can chuckle at your imperfections as a preacher as well as you can chuckle at the inconsistencies of others, you may know that Truth has been no stranger in that particular situation.

C. In the pulpit-preaching situation *noise disrupts* and causes Truth a bad time. That *noise* may actually be a physical noise. Joe Johnson tells about this *noise* in a funny way, but it was not funny when it happened.

179

While a ministerial student, I journeyed out to another station which was meeting in a home. Upon my return, my mother asked me, "Son, how did it go?" I replied, "Mom, we had 106 present."

Mom exulted, "Why, that's wonderful, son." To which I responded, "Yep, 106—six human beings and 100 baby chicks." Verily, those gospel birds drowned out my message. Since that time I've carried on a personal vendetta against all grown chickens. I've devoured as many of them as possible.[113]

You preach in a church where the flushing of a commode across the hall can be heard, and you have the ingredients of unplanned humor.

I've pastored more than one church where there's a steady procession of kids availing themselves of the church's water-related facilities. I suggested to a certain music director that we consider having five or six interludes, complete with "Pomp and Circumstance" and the processional from "Aida," during every service. Half of that church's budget was dedicated to the water bill.

So help me, this happened to a friend of mine. He was presenting the invitation at the close of the service. A teen-age girl pushed into the aisle and sauntered toward my friend.

With unbridled joy, he met her five giant steps up the aisle. Clasping her hand, he emotionally asked, "My dear, why do you come today?"

She tersely replied, "Preacher, would you please let me by. I gotta use the rest room." [114]

That *noise* may be audience preoccupation with a wasp flying about, unlighted candles on the altar, an usher looking for the mother of a baby crying in the nursery, audience fatigue, audience attention span, or audience belief that humor does not belong in church. Or the noise might be the preacher's lack of preparation, the preacher's bad pulpit manners, poor use of the language, absence of forgiveness, etc. An intuitive feeling that the planned humor will not work when the time to preach arrives may in itself be a *noise*. The feeling defies analysis. But Truth says, "Don't use it." In Part V, we discussed whether you could plan to have a sense of humor and concluded that you could only if first you knew you alone could not. But you with God could see together incongruities before the sermon is preached. You could plan where the humor would fit the best; i.e., in the introduction to gain attention (with something relevant to the thesis of the sermon), in illustrations of points for recall of those points, and for a release of tension that inevitably builds in people when Truths are proclaimed. And now comes another answer to that question, "Can you *plan* to have a sense of humor?" When the time comes for you to put to use that planned humor, be ready to forget it if the situation is not as you had planned it to be. Too often I have fallen into the trap of planning some perfect humor—only to have it (and me!) flop! When humor seems to be that "good," it probably is not!

I felt the trap door beneath me open slowly as I told this story: "One day a father found his young son petting a strange dog. The father yelled, 'Get away from that dirty animal! You might catch a disease from him.'

" 'But Daddy,' the boy pleaded.

" 'He's a good-for-nothing!' the father replied. 'Mangy, skinny, dirty, and his leg is hurt.'

" 'I know,' the boy said, his eyes filled with concern. 'But see, he wags his tail real good.' "

As I write this down, and re-think my plan to use it, the story still looks good enough to keep in the plan. At the particular moment, it simply did not work. This says: as you plan to use humor, plan also not to use it if you do not feel right about it when the times comes to preach. Truth can "tell" you the conditions conducive to humor (to gain attention, to retain attention, to illustrate, etc.). You write down those "Truths" in the outline of the sermon. But when you preach, the Truth that monitors and interprets all the variables in a given situation may nudge you to drop that "Truth" that you earlier worked into the sermon outline. This *drop* does not negate the written Truth earlier included. It affirms the overall Truth you entered in your plans—your plan *not* to use it if need be. Truth is always relevant to the moment that you write the sermon, to the moment you preach it, to the *Now*.

While I can see how Truth works in the aforementioned manner, I cannot explain how it was not right to use that illustration. When the planned time came to tell it, something was not right. I "heard" a *noise*. Another day, another moment, maybe yes. But not that time. *When in doubt about using humor, don't!*

In some cases, humor can help overcome the noise. A loud sneeze during a sermon's crucial pause can cause low-keyed snickers. An "Amen" by the preacher following the sneeze causes a laughter that helps him regain "control" of the situation. In other cases humor fails (remember, when in doubt, do not use it). If you stand in the pulpit unprepared, your efforts at humor become a bad joke. Bad pulpit manners, like picking your nose, or scratching your head, make for laughs, but not the kind you want.

If you think you are funny, you may not be in the minds of your audience. Sometimes we mistakenly think our actions funny. Our stories are not funny if we are not seeing the incongruities of the funny-looking episodes or the humor by surprise, and telling what we see. Rather, we become to the audience an incongruity. They see and laugh (though some-

182

what nervously) at us as we attempt to tell the humor. It is not what we say that is funny, but who we are as we say it. The incongruity the audience sees is this: they see us thinking we are funny when we are not. They laugh at that horrendous mistake we make.

We take ourselves too seriously, and unwittingly become humorous in the process. This is the kind of laughter we do not need! This laughter is at our foolishness, and not our sense of humor. A young preacher told a story in his sermon. The people laughed. He then told something that he intended to be taken seriously. They laughed at it too. He told them that what he had said was not funny. From that point on nothing he said was funny. He lost his audience for any use of humor. He just lost his audience, period.

1. In most cases *a laugh at yourself* in that moment when you make your mistake *helps you recapture the audience* for you. This works best when you are held in high esteem. The greater the authority of the preacher in the mind of the audience, the better the self-put-down for the preacher works. The disparity between the high public position and the ordinary human status that comes off in the put-down accounts for the humor. That kind of humor rewards the preacher with higher credibility in the mind of the audience. After that revelation of Truth through humor, the audience will be more open to the *straight* gospel that the preacher proclaims. The following illustrations show how this worked to build credibility for two prominent preachers.

When Bishop Robert E. Goodrich, Jr., preached in our church, he started with this introduction:

A little church out from St. Louis, about thirty miles out, I guess, was without a pastor for nearly three months. We simply had nobody to send. And the chairman of their Board had to get a preacher each Sunday. He did real fine until finally he came down to one Sun-

183

day and he couldn't get one. He called me along about Friday. And explained to me the situation. And then he asked me if by any chance I could come preach. I looked it up and told him by chance it would be possible. I went out there on Sunday morning. When he introduced me, he told the people the situation. And then he said, "Of course, we would have been glad to have someone of lesser ability. But we couldn't find one." [115]

Bishop William Cannon, a bachelor bishop in the Methodist Church, tells this on himself. He said, "When my friends were running me for bishop, they told me my chances to be elected would be much better if I found me a wife.

"I told them, 'But what would I do with her if I am not elected!' "

This self-put-down works only if you are "up" in the minds of your audience. The disparity between your authority in their minds and the low blow you have delivered to yourself accounts for the humor. If in their minds you are already low enough, a self-deprecating comment from you would only support their low opinion of you.

2. McLuhan, for example, contends that simply the nature of the medium—the way each structures and presents information—influences the way we perceive the world.[116]

McLuhan's The Medium Is the Message adapts well to this model of the pulpit-preaching situation and helps you see why you must laugh at yourself too. The medium for Truth is the whole situation: the two transceivers (the preacher and the audience) plus the *noise*. When all that blends together, the totality is the message. The audience with its expectations *is* the message. The environment with its influences *is* the message. The preacher *is* the message. The Bible that is used in planning and preaching *is* the message. The Truth above all that is going on tells that each of these inputs *is* the message. That humor, exposed by Truth through the audience, the surroundings, and the preacher *is not* the message, but points to the message. And it always plays that supportive role. This way of looking at the pulpit-preaching situation puts the preacher as well as the audience under the judgment of Truth. This awareness of this-is-the-way-it-works keeps the preacher from looking down at his audience in a condescending or paternalistic humor. He laughs at others and himself.

3. *If your audience misses your humor,* forget it, and go on with your sermon. They took it straight, and likely a congruent Truth got through to them. Why bother about their miss? The purpose for your humor finally is to point to the congruent expression of Truth.

4. *If your audience catches some humor that you did not intend, keep the sermon moving.*

Words with double meanings can make for a humor, a *noise,* that does not belong in the pulpit. The humor does not serve the purpose of the worship setting. For instance, the host preacher, for whom I was preaching a Revival, made his announcements and then began calling on the pew captains to give the number of persons who filled their pews. After going through the list of pew captains, Miss Essie, a well-known old maid, had the largest number in attendance. The preacher then asked the question that he wishes a thousand times he had back: "Is there anybody here who can top Miss Essie?" Most of the adults never heard the goof. Some teenagers did. The preacher handled this *noise* perfectly when he moved right on as if nothing happened.

When you plan your sermon, do not plan to use words with double meanings. When you do stumble into using one unintentionally, do not recognize what you have done. You interpret the word straight, and keep the sermon moving. If you recognize what you have done, you have lost your audience (you may have lost them anyway!).

5. *The preacher whose humor tends to run away with him must be doubly careful* not to let this happen when the time comes to preach. If he does, his humor becomes a *noise*. As an end rather than a means, it drowns the purpose of the sermon. A preacher plagued with a freewheeling sense of humor came to a district preacher's meeting to preach a sermon challenging the group in the area of evangelism. With humor he got audience attention; with humor he made his points. Then he buried his points with ludicrous stories. With humor he concluded the "sermon." Not one congruent Truth came from this "sermon." Later he asked the host District Superintendent, "How did I do?" The District Superintendent said, "You missed a good chance to preach the gospel!" The guest preacher agreed. He had a problem: his freewheeling sense of humor made him more a stand-up comic than a preacher, more a *noise* than a channel of Truth.

6. Many times when a *noise* occurs during the preaching of a sermon, *a simple expression of Truth offers humorous relief.* The disturbance causes the incongruity. The straight situation is disrupted. A simple expression of Truth explodes the contained energy that needs to be released. When the lights went out while he was preaching his sermon, one preacher simply stated a Truth: "You have not been struck blind. The lights are out." The people laughed nervously. After a short pause he said, "I've got some good sermon notes here. But I can't see to read them." The people laughed again. By this time some candles were lit, and soon the lights were back on.

To combat that *noise* the preacher simply told the Truth. This expression of the Truth may be taken straight or funny by the audience. That means this method of dealing with *noise* always works.

7. Truth in the time of preaching may negate the planned humor, or alter it in a way that it is acceptable under the unplanned conditions. Or *the noise may dictate that nothing be changed.* For instance, the recently graduated seminarian

186

was delivering his first sermon to an audience of the elderly in a Rest Home. He was reading his manuscript when one of his listeners "went to the bathroom" right there. Someone went for a nurse. He preached on. The nurse came across in front of him to inspect the situation. He preached on. She then went for the orderly. He came into the room and began mopping up there in front of the young preacher as the nurse led the relieved lady to her room. The young preacher, with eyes glued to his manuscript, never missed a beat! He delivered it just as he had planned it. The humor he had planned was given and not laughed at. He said that he was not sure they heard the sermon! That interruption was a *noise*. But had he tried to do anything other than carry on as he did, the *noise* would have been *louder*.

What could you do with the following *noise?* In a small East Texas church the preacher, who had come from "high church" Presbyterianism, was preaching in a rural United Methodist worship service. His liturgy moved very smoothly until he came to the doxology (a new innovation to that congregation). The pianist simply could not get the timing right. She hit the notes while she should have been holding a beat longer on the last ones—she added a few sounds that were not written in and left out some that were. Finally, right in the middle of it all, while people were putting forth every effort to praise God, she piped out louder than the piano music and the singing: "I'm sure messin' up, ain't I!"

How do you handle that *noise?*—All you *can* do is keep the liturgy moving. And hope that time will take care of that *noise*. Before that occurs probably another *noise* will come into the situation! Anyway there are some *noises* you leave alone because your effort to set things right could be louder than the *noise* you try to correct.

8. *An explained joke* loses its humor (unless the "explanation" is given in a ludicrous manner), and *becomes a noise.* This means the preacher never tries to explain a joke. If the

187

audience does not catch the humor, forget it. Go on with the sermon. An effort to try to explain the humor would only evoke a sympathetic embarrassment from a red-faced audience. You can see the audience "digging a hole" when the preacher said in an effort to explain his joke: "Don't you get it?" And then he tries to help them "get it." The *noise* became unbearable.

9. If the preacher uses his humor to show off, his *showiness becomes a noise.*

It costs much to put aside the alluring reputation of an orator or a philosopher, for the calling of a herald. That means he resists the temptation to preach showily great sermons. Kipling has pictured the devil's supreme temptation in the field of art. When the caveman was daubing his first painting, the devil asked, "It's pretty, but is it art?" To the preacher, the devil's most seductive word is the word "great." The devil whispers between the pages of the sermon manuscript, "Oh, it may be useful, of course, but is it *great?*" To every preacher, the devil brings the third temptation of Jesus, with enticing contemporary trimmings. He says, "Do something dazzling. Forget about serving people. That's rather ordinary stuff. Fling yourself from the pinnacle of the Temple. Dazzle them. Get yourself a reputation. You can be immortal." In such a time, remember that noble figure of Greek mythology, Chiron, who was willing to give up his chance of immortality to save Prometheus. There is a New Testament echo of that. The preacher must be willing to forgo his immortality, his reputation, if by any means he may save some.[117]

That showiness *noise* can be *heard* and you do not have to say a word.

Brethren, I admonish you to dress tastefully. One of my preacher friends has exceedingly tasteful attire. His ties and shirts are full of gravy, eggs, and coffee.

If you lack confidence in your preaching, wear outlandish clothes, and the zanier the better. When you don Mafia sunglasses indoors, a vermilion shirt, and fuchsia tie, fire-engine-red trousers, and patriotic shoes, they're not going to hear your sermon anyway.[118]

The many noises make it difficult for the Truth to reach the congregation (or the preacher!). And *that* is the Truth. Just to recognize how difficult it is to know the Truth gives you a revelation that many preachers have never received. That openness to Divine Truth transmits to the congregation in spite of the many *noises.* You can never conquer all *noises.* But your faith in God's Truth diminishes all *noises* to the insignificance they represent. Your good humor helps you rise above the *noises.*

Be careful at this point. If you think that you have put yourself above the *noises* by your exceptional talent for humor, you may look like a proud peacock to the congregation. They may be laughing *at* you. That unintended humor can send your credibility tumbling. When it does, a laugh at yourself can start the credibility-building process again.

Anybody can laugh at others. But can you laugh at yourself? If you can, you are ready to risk the use of humor.

D. *The use of humor is risky business.* If someone in the congregation is too close to the tragic dimension of the humor, your humor may alienate him. On one occasion I illustrated a point with a comment I heard from a pall bearer while enroute to a burial. He joked with one of the other pall bearers when he said: "Paul, you are lagging on the handle." I referred to that funeral-procession comment when I said in my sermon: "In this life somebody is always lagging on the handle." That light humor seemed innocent enough until my eyes turned to the sad eyes of a young lady who is dying with cancer. Others smiled. She didn't. I will never use that illustration again. But I will stumble into similar mistakes as long as I use humor. As long as you use humor, you take risks.

You may fail in your humor. But your humor will ultimately work for good if you remember that humor is used to serve the Truth that reveals the incongruity in the first place. A particular incongruity comes and goes. Old jokes told over and over lose their humor. Truth is no longer served. Eternal significance is not given to a temporary incongruity, but to the Eternal God who is Truth.

1. *Your sense of humor will be less risky in the pulpit-preaching situation if it is a part of your prayer life.*

> *The subject-object prayer model in itself is ludicrous. Imagine the hubris* of one who prays to God as if God were an object. It is a funny sight that shows prayer is not as it ought to be. A glimpse of that incongruity can be the beginning of a vital prayer life. First, it can open one to listen to God in prayer, to let the power of God's being come in and make one feel one *is* accepted, *is* somebody. Then one becomes in this relationship with God *to be* in the spirit of prayer. Out of that spirit one may or may not talk, but one will always be *with it.* One may moan, shout for joy, cry; and as long as one is in the spirit of prayer, one may "pray to God" with the assurance that God was there before a word was spoken.[119]

When you see yourself as the bumbling, stumbling self you are, you depend on God for support as you plan your sermon. That dependency on God comes through as you stand in the pulpit-preaching situation. A right use of humor reveals a dependency on God. You never laugh at that dependency. But you laugh with that dependency on God at man's incongruities. And that includes your own! Without a prayerful dependency on God while in the pulpit, you would take yourself too seriously, try to defend yourself, explain your mistake, and lose your audience in the process. Prayer precedes you into the pulpit. It goes with you into the pulpit. And hopefully it saves you while you are there.

Prayer wedded to a sense of humor does not do away with all risks. To live is to risk. But it does assure an attitude that can better deal with the risk. To use no humor is a risk; would the risk of seriousness or humor better deal with this situation that happened to Joe Johnson?

> I was preaching a revival meeting in a country church (haven't preached too many elsewhere) and waxing eloquent, enchanted by my voice. As I developed point seven, a first-grade boy blurted out, "Mama, why doesn't that fat man sit down, and shut up and let the pastor preach?" Point seven evaporated.[120]

Any gesture without a sense of humor would be a rebuke of that boy, of that mama, of that congregation whose sympathies lie with the lad, of the best in the preacher himself, of the Truth that illumined the incongruity. The risk of a serious reaction on the part of a preacher in a similar situation is far greater than the risk of humor.

The awareness of this particular Truth on the part of the preacher overcomes enough of the *noises* in the pulpit-preaching situation to allow the Truth via the message to be experienced by both transceivers, the preacher and the audience.

2. Remember that you are not the only one in the pulpit-preaching situation who takes a risk. *The audience risks too.* They risk that you will have nothing to say. No message. No sense of their sense of humor. They risk that you will become a *noise* to them.

3. *So what do you do?* *Preach your faith in God who takes the biggest risk* of all. Make His venture in your preaching one of the best "days" in His Life. You may know that He is with you just like He was with me that day several years ago when I had been fore-warned that a pulpit committee from a large church was coming to hear me preach. I pulled out my best candy stick sermon. I had preached it in that church. But it was so good I preached it again on that Sunday that the people from the big church were to come—and didn't! As I preached, I kept looking for them to come in. I added a few points here and there to prolong the sermon. I saved the best part of the sermon for them.

But nobody showed. I preached an entire sermon to an audience who never arrived.

To add insult to injury, one of the parishioners said upon leaving, "I liked it better the first time you preached it!"

After all had gone, I poked my head out the front door. Nobody was there. I walked through the sanctuary to my office. I looked around. I could have sworn I heard Someone laughing. When I realized Who He was, we both laughed at me together.

By grace He saves us through faith—and a good sense of humor.

POSTSCRIPT

POSTSCRIPT

There is no authority (except Truth) on the subject of humor-and-the-preacher. About the time you begin to feel secure in your use of humor, you will fail and probably blame your audience for not having enough sense to see your good humor! That moment challenges you to admit that your ignorance misjudged the mental posture of your audience. If the audience does not see your humor, the fault is not theirs. It is yours.

And you can learn from it. Truth calls you to learn from your mistakes. A preacher makes his biggest mistake when he thinks he can use humor wisely without forgiveness of sin. Without forgiveness, the preacher justifies his sins. A preacher who justifies his sin will justify all manner of humor misuse.

A re-reading of Part I offers the best conclusion to this book. That puts you back to where humor *is*—inside you where God's Truth illumines for you incongruities. Humor is God's business; God's business is serious business. "He who sits in the heavens laughs." [121] Your audience who sits in the pews will too, if you who stand in the pulpit sense the humor God's Truth exposes. And learn when and how to say what you sense.

While you can learn how to use humor, you will never be able to evaluate your humor objectively. You cannot evaluate anything *objectively*. Your best objective thinking has too much of the subject (yourself!) in it.

The best *objective* thinking by others *about* you has too much of themselves in what they say. This is true no matter how "honest" they feel in their evaluation about you. The honesty syndrome transcends denominational lines in the laity and the pastoral ministry. There are pastors, secure in their position, who enjoy the ego trip of being told by a hand-picked "evaluation committee" that they are doing a fine job. Naturally, the pastor has to arrange to have one or two "nit-pickers" on the committee who will be "honest" with him and tell him he could use fewer gestures but more excitement in his preaching; more time spent on visitation, but don't call during the day, during the dinner hour (6:00-8:00 P.M.), or after 9:00 P.M.; less time spent with his family, but be a family man; less time spent in the study, but come up with better sermons; less expensive clothing, but be a good dresser; and so on with the list of "honest" grievances.

Shove your tongue firmly in your cheek and read on. If you have a multi-staff, and want to get a staff person straightened out, then do the same thing with your staff. First you must be sure that the staff really knows who is the boss, and then set up the one you, and the majority of the staff, know is lagging behind in his/her duties. An "honest" confession by you starts this process beautifully. "I must admit I have not given you the time that you needed, etc." You know and the staff knows how far they can go in agreeing with you. If they are smart, they will say, "You surely are 'honest' to admit this." They know they have pleased you in saying this. The end result is: they have clobbered the one whom you would not confront in a more private conversation.

This navel-gazing "honesty" syndrome robs the pastor of his prophetic calling. His proclamation changes from "Thus

196

saith the Lord" to "Thus saith the Evaluation Committee."
Can you hear Jesus calling together an evaluation committee
who would help Him set his goals? Can you hear Paul before
Festus and Agrippa saying: "Sirs, I have an evaluation report of my ministry that shows you what a fine job I am
doing representing Christ"? Can you hear *any* disciple meeting the challenges of his hour with an evaluation report? (A
closer look reveals that evaluation committees crucified
Christ and asked for Paul's head!)

One church I was sent to had an evaluation committee to
put down on paper what they wanted in their new minister.
They sent this list of items to the Bishop. He wrote them
back a nice letter with this answer to their evaluation of what
their minister ought to be: "St. Paul could not fill the re-
quirements you have listed. But I am sending you Bob Parrott—!"

Very few evaluation committees today would want even
St. Paul. He was called of God to a prophetic ministry. And
he would hardly sit still for such strange game-playing.

While we are talking about St. Paul, let us hear what he
says about the matter: "We *are* fools for Christ's sake, but
you *are* wise in Christ! We *are* weak, but you *are* strong! You
are distinguished, but we *are* dishonored!—For though you
might have ten thousand instructors in Christ, yet *you do* not
have many fathers; for in Christ Jesus I have begotten you
through the gospel." [122]

A fool for Christ is difficult for anyone to evaluate. The
reason is simple. He/she is motivated from deep within—
from faith. Only One traffics in that territory of judgment.

The "bottom line" simply is: no two persons view any one
preacher in precisely the same way. Any evaluation of any
minister is a distortion of the Truth, whether it is a "good" or
"bad" evaluation.

How then can a preacher know he/she is fulfilling his/her
call to ministry? How can there be a true evaluation? *Be* in

tune with Being-itself. Know that your gaps exist (at no time are you completely who you ought to be), and that God loves you anyway. That deep sense of God's acceptance of you permits you to take criticism without that criticism destroying your sense of self-integrity. I have found that my worst critics help me know the Truth of my human brokenness. They heighten my awareness of the tragic weakness of this brokenness that we call sin. That serves for my good. I put my faith in God, not man. Clay-footed men can mislead you in their evaluations. But not God.

This *being*-in-tune with Truth will show your incongruities. God can use others' comments to help you see your incongruities. Can help you laugh at yourself—and at your critics who act like little gods in making their comments. Usually they see themselves above making your mistakes. They are ludicrous even as you. The one who benefits from this laugh is the one who recognizes his/her gap, and goes on with God's acceptance.

Committees set goals for you. God motivates you. You may not know what end God has in mind, but you will know what He has placed in your heart and mind. Where you end is not important. That you go with Him is important. Listen for thoughts from the Supreme Intelligence. Grab hold of those mental images and heart nudges, and plan in God's time frame to do the best with what God has given you. Carry out those dreams of God as far as your time within these human conditions permits.

This is not a matter of your sitting down and setting goals that you, by your own "supreme" intelligence, have created for God's sake, but a matter of permitting God to give you something to work on. Your own goal-setting sets you up for a fall. *You* fail when your goal is frustrated. God's movements in directing your life day by day may to others look like a failure at times. Your achievements do not fit their goals for you. But to you the "failure" (usually recognized by an "evaluation" committee of one or more) is but a step in faith. You've learned from it. You've learned that this particular plan may not work. That is a positive experience. Faith in God's Grace ultimately takes care of all negatives (non-being) in that forward-moving manner. And humor at self and others remains a vital part of the process.

This book infinitely misses being the last word on the subject of the preacher's humor. Any entertainment that it is the "last word" would be ludicrous. The book affirms that God has a sense of humor, and a preacher can have a sense of humor too.

NOTES

1. Marie Collins Swakey, *Comic Laughter* (New Haven and London: Yale University Press, 1961), pp. 12-13.
2. Max Eastman, *Enjoyment of Laughter* (New York: Simon & Schuster, 1936), p. 9, 2a, ibid., p. 304.
3. Lecture given by Malcolm Muggeridge in First United Methodist Church, Longview, Texas.
4. Stephen Leacock, *Humor In Theory and Technique* (New York: Dodd, Mead, Inc., 1935), p. 15.
5. Victor Frankl, *Man's Search for Meaning* (New York: Washington Square Press, 1964), pp. 68-69.
6. Eastman, *op. cit.*, p. 41.
7. Bob Parrott, *Ontology of Humor* (New York: Philosophical Library Publishers, 1981), pp. 16-17.
8. Psalms 2:4.
9. George E. Sweazey, *Preaching the Good News* (Englewood Cliffs, New Jersey: Prentice-Hall, 1976), p. 206.
10. Webb B. Garrison, *The Preacher and His Audience* (Westwood, New Jersey: Fleming H. Revell Company, 1954), p. 192.
11. *Ibid.*, p. 205.
12. Parrott, *op. cit.*, p. 37.
13. Swakey, *op. cit.*, p. 16.
14. Ecclesiastes 7:6.

15. Arthur E. Hoyt, *The Preacher, His Person, Message, and Method* (New York: Hodder & Stoughton, 1909), p. 128.
16. Garrison, *op. cit.*, p. 195.
17. James H. Robinson, *Adventurous Preaching* (Great Neck, New York: Channel Press, 1956), p. 19.
18. Proverbs 17:22.
19. Thomas F. Chilcote, Jr., *The Excellence of Our Calling* (New York: E. P. Dutton & Company, 1954), p. 41.
20. I John 4:8.
21. I Corinthians 13:8.
22. Hoyt, *op. cit.*, pp. 368-369.
23. Swakey, *op. cit.*, p. 96.
24. Leonard Feinberg, *Introduction To Satire* (Ames, Iowa: Iowa State University Press, 1967), p. 7.
25. Parrott, *op. cit.*, p. 22.
26. Mark 7:9.
27. Parrott, *op. cit.*, p. 18.
28. John 14:6.
29. Parrott, *op. cit.*, p. 17.
30. Nelvin Voss, *For God's Sake, Laugh!* (Richmond, Va.: John Knox Press, 1952), p. 24.
31. Dudley Zuver, *Salvation by Laughter* (New York: Harper & Brothers, 1933), p. 146.
32. Mark 4:21.
33. Matthew 25:1-13.
34. Matthew 11:7-8.
35. Luke 16:3.
36. Matthew 6:16.
37. Matthew 23:5-7.
38. Matthew 11:17.
39. Matthew 6:24.
40. Luke 18:10-11.
41. Luke 14:7-11.
42. Matthew 7:3-5.
43. Luke 15:18-20.
44. Matthew 7:6.
45. Mark 10:25.
46. Matthew 23:24.

47. Zuver, *op. cit.*, p. 89.
48. I Peter 2:21.
49. Keith W. Jennison, *The Humorous Mr. Lincoln* (New York: Bonanza Books, 1965), pp. 4-5.
50. Parrott, *op. cit.*, p. vii.
51. Psalm 27:14.
52. Jonah 2:1-9.
53. Exodus 32:32.
54. Acts 12:16.
55. John 17:17.
56. Luke 22:32.
57. Matthew 19:17.
58. Romans 8:26.
59. Parrott, *op, cit.*, p. 21.
60. *Ibid.*, p. 5.
61. John 8:32.
62. Parrott, *op. cit.*, pp. 65-66.
63. S. I. Hayakawa, *Language In Thought and Action,* 3rd ed. (New York: Harcourt Brace Jovanovich, 1972), p. 151.
64. Albert C. Outler, *Psychotherapy and the Christian Message* (New York: Harper & Brothers, 1954), p. 180.
65. Rollo May, *The Meaning of Anxiety* (New York: The Ronald Press Company, 1950), p. 13.
66. Outler, *op. cit.*, p. 180.
67. Wayne Oates, *An Introduction to Pastoral Counseling* (Nashville-Broadman Press, 1959), p. vi.
68. Howard Clinebell, *Basic Types of Pastoral Counseling* (Nashville: Abingdon Press, 1966), p. 61.
69. Sidney Jourard, *The Transparent Self* (Princeton, N.J.: Van Nostrand, 1964), pp. 59-65.
70. Massey Hamilton Shepherd, Jr., *The Living Liturgy* (New York: Oxford University Press, 1946), p. 12.
71. Douglas Horton, *The Meaning of Worship* (New York, Harper & Brothers, 1959), p. 40.
72. Parrott, *op. cit.*, p. 38.
73. Paul Tillich, *Systematic Theology,* Vol. 11 (Chicago: University of Chicago Press, 1952), pp. 50-51.
74. Parrott, *op. cit.*, p. 16.

75. Matthew 18:20.
76. G. David Mortensen, *Communication: The Study of Human Interaction* (New York: McGraw-Hill Book Co., 1972), p. 135.
77. Parrott, *op. cit.*, p. 66.
78. James F. White, *New Forms of Worship* (Nashville: Abingdon Press, 1971), p. 40.
79. Parrott, *op. cit.*, p. 36.
80. Ibid., p. 67.
81. Ibid., p. 18.
82. R. G. Lee, *Payday Everyday* (Nashville, Tennessee: Broadman Press, 1947), pp. 106-107.
83. Sweazey, *op. cit.*, pp. 208-209.
84. *Ibid.*, p. 208.
85. *Ibid.*, p. 210.
86. *Ibid.*, p. 209.
87. Proverbs 11:22.
88. Proverbs 25:19.
89. Proverbs 26:18-19.
90. Proverbs 27:15-16.
91. Isaiah 28:20.
92. Isaiah 44:14-17.
93. Mark 7:9.
94. Matthew 7:3.
95. Matthew 25:24.
96. Matthew 11:16-17.
97. Jonah.
98. Esther.
99. Halford E. Luccock, *The Acts of the Apostles In Present Day Preaching* (Chicago and New York: Willett, Clark & Co., 1939), p. 74.
100. Taped sermon of Dr. R. G. Lee.
101. R. G. Lee, *Bed of Pearls* (Nashville, Tennessee: Broadman Press, 1936), pp. 95-97.
102. R. G. Lee, *Grapes from Gospel Vines* (Nashville, Tennessee: Broadman Press, 1976), p. 109.
103. R. G. Lee, *Heart to Heart* (Nashville, Tennessee: Broadman Press, 1977), p. 55.

104. *Ibid.*, p. 118.
105. Halford E. Luccock, *Jesus and the American Mind* (New York, Cincinnati, Chicago: The Abingdon Press, 1930), pp. 114-115.
106. Halford E. Luccock, *Acts of the Apostles In Present Day Preaching* (New York: Willett, Clark & Co., 1939), p. 150.
107. George E. Sweazey, *Preaching the Good News* (Englewood Cliffs, New Jersey: Prentice-Hall, 1976), p. 206.
108. Joe Johnson, *Preacher, You're the Best Pasture We've Ever Had* (Nashville: Broadman, 1972), p. 9.
109. James C. McCroskey, *An Introduction to Rhetorical Communication*, 2nd ed. (Englewood Cliffs, New Jersey: Prentice-Hall Inc., 1972), pp. 48-49.
110. Johnson, *op. cit.*, p. 23.
111. Frederick Buechner, *Telling the Truth—The Gospel as Tragedy, Comedy and Fairy Tale* (San Francisco: Harper and Row, Publishers, 1977), p. 8.
112. Halford E. Luccock, "Humor and Religion—I" in *The Christian Century*, February 17, 1960, p. 207.
113. Johnson, *op. cit.*, p. 14.
114. *Ibid.*, p. 26.
115. Sermon preached by Bishop Robert E. Goodrich in Longview First United Methodist Church.
116. Edited by Wilbur Schramm and Donald F. Roberts, *The Process and Effects of Mass Communication* (Urbana, Chicago, and London: University of Illinois Press, 1972), p. 386.
117. Halford E. Luccock, *Communicating the Gospel* (New York: Harper and Brothers Publishers, 1954), p. 44.
118. Johnson, *op. cit.*, p. 25.
119. Parrott, *op. cit.*, p. 55.
120. Johnson, *op. cit.*, p. 29.
121. Psalm 2:4.
122. I Corinthians 4:10.